# The Monetary Theory of Production

In mainstream economic theory money functions as an instrument for the circulation of commodities or for keeping a stock of liquid wealth. In neither case is it considered fundamental to the production of goods or the distribution of income. Augusto Graziani challenges traditional theories of monetary production, arguing that a modern economy based on credit cannot be understood without a focus on the administration of credit flows. He argues that market asset configuration depends not upon consumer preferences and available technologies but on how money and credit are managed. A strong exponent of the circulation theory of monetary production, Graziani presents an original and perhaps controversial argument which will stimulate debate on the topic.

**Augusto Graziani** is Professor of Economics in the University of Rome La Sapienza. He is the author of *Teoria Economica* (4th edition, 2002).

T0340289

**Federico Caffè Lectures**

This series of annual lectures was initiated to honour the memory of Federico Caffè. They are jointly sponsored by the Department of Public Economics at the University of Rome, where Caffè held a chair from 1959 to 1987, and the Bank of Italy, where he served for many years as an adviser. The publication of the lectures will provide a vehicle for leading scholars in the economics profession, and for the interested general reader, to reflect on the pressing economic and social issues of the times.

# The Monetary Theory of Production

**Augusto Graziani**

CAMBRIDGE UNIVERSITY PRESS

CAMBRIDGE UNIVERSITY PRESS
Cambridge, New York, Melbourne, Madrid, Cape Town, Singapore, São Paulo, Delhi

Cambridge University Press
The Edinburgh Building, Cambridge CB2 8RU, UK

Published in the United States of America by Cambridge University Press, New York

www.cambridge.org
Information on this title: www.cambridge.org/9780521104173

First published 2003
This digitally printed version 2009

A catalogue record for this publication is available from the British Library

Library of Congress Cataloguing in Publication data
Graziani, Augusto.
The monetary theory of production / Augusto Graziani.
    p.   cm. – (Cambridge studies in international relations ; 92) (Federico
Caffè lectures)
Includes bibliographical references and index.
ISBN 0-521-81211-9
1. Money.   2. Production (Economic theory)   I. Title.   II. Series.
III. Series: Federico Caffè lectures
HG220.A2G66   2003
332.4′01 – dc21   2003043963

ISBN 978-0-521-81211-5 hardback
ISBN 978-0-521-10417-3 paperback

# Contents

# Contents

# Acknowledgements

The present book reproduces, in an expanded and revised version, the content of two lectures given in December 1998 in the Faculty of Economics of the University of Rome La Sapienza, in the framework of the series of yearly lectures dedicated to the memory of Federico Caffè. A first synthetic presentation of the same ideas was published in 1989 as *The Theory of the Monetary Circuit*, in the Thames Papers in Political Economy series. A subsequent enlarged version was published in Italian as *La teoria monetaria della produzione* (Arezzo, Banca Popolare dell'Etruria, 1994).

Thanks are due to the Faculty of Economics at the University of Rome La Sapienza, and in particular to my colleagues Domenico Tosato and Mario Tiberi, for inviting me to give these lectures. Special thanks are due to Philip Arestis, at the time editor of the Thames Papers in Political Economy, who in 1988 first encouraged me to contribute a paper on the theory of the monetary circuit.

*Rome, May 2002*

# Acknowledgments

# 1

# Introduction

## 1.1 The theory of the monetary circuit

Over the last twenty years, mostly owing to research carried out by French and Italian scholars, a new formulation of monetary macroeconomics, the so-called 'Theory of the monetary circuit', also denominated 'The circulation approach' (Deleplace and Nell 1996), has been gaining ground. The basic theoretical tenets of the theory can be synthesised in three main propositions: rigorous distinction between banks and firms, endogenous determination of the money stock, and rejection of the marginal theory of distribution.[1]

### *The circulation approach in the early Swedish and German literatures*

Under a strictly chronological criterion, the first description of a monetary circuit is found in Knut Wicksell's rightly celebrated monograph on *Interest and Prices*.[2]

---

[1] A general presentation of the circuit approach is contained in Lavoie 1987, Graziani 1989, Halevi and Taouil 1998. An implicit description of the circuit mechanism can be found in Bossone 2001. An excellent review and critical assessment of the post-Keynesian reading of the macroeconomic model is given by Arestis 1997, chapter 3. A detailed analysis of the concept of endogenous money and of the debate between accommodationists (supporters of endogenous money) and structuralists (accepting endogenous money only under severe qualifications) is contained in Fontana 2001.

[2] Wicksell 1936 [1898], chapter 9, section B. In Wicksell's wake, the Swedish school has analysed the monetary circulation along the same

Wicksell's analysis strongly influenced a number of authors belonging to the Austrian and German schools, both having a long tradition in the analysis of money and banking.[3] The very term 'circuit', introduced in contemporary literature by French authors, reproduces the German *Kreislauf*, a term used by German writers to describe the circulation of money and of real goods (Schumpeter 1934 [1911], chapter 1). Neisser devoted two works to the analysis of money circulation. The first one (Neisser 1928) gives ample space to the relationships between banks and firms. The second one (Neisser 1931) is specifically devoted to the analysis of circulation among firms and between firms and wage earners. N. Johannsen, the famous amateur economist recalled by Keynes in the *Treatise on Money* (1971 [1930], chapter 27), analyses in detail the monetary circuit in his book *The Circuit of Money* published in 1903 under the pseudonym of J.J.O. Lahn (an analysis of Johannsen's book is contained in Hagemann and Rühl 1987). The German contributions to the analysis of the circular flow between the 1930s and the 1960s are analysed in detail by Schmitt and Greppi (1996).

More recently, a revival of the circulation approach in Germany has been carried out by the so-called School of Monetary Keynesianism, headed by Hajo Riese in Berlin. The Berlin school describes the market mechanism as a monetary circuit, rejects the marginal theory of distribution and defines money as an institutional entity and not as a spontaneous product of the market (Lüken Klassen 1998; Riese 1998).

lines (Lundberg 1937). The 'Introduction' by L. Berti to the Italian edition of Myrdal 1939 is an excellent guide to the Swedish monetary theory considered in this perspective.

[3] Schumpeter 1934 [1911]; von Mises 1934 [1912]; Hahn 1920; Neisser 1928, 1931 and 1950 [1934]; Schneider 1962, chapter 2. A detailed analysis of Schumpeter's monetary thought is contained in Messori 1984. De Vecchi 1993 is a most important piece of research centred on works written by Schumpeter before he moved to the United States.

## The circulation approach in France

In many aspects, the French school of the circuit had a precursor in an isolated French scholar, Jacques Le Bourva. To him is due one of the first and more lucid presentations of the monetary circuit as well as of the process of money creation and destruction, both viewed as endogenous phenomena (Le Bourva 1962; reprinted with a 'Comment' by Marc Lavoie 1992).

More recently, the revival and analytical development of circuit theory in France has been due to three main groups of authors. The so-called Dijon school is headed by Bernard Schmitt, an author who has given a precise formulation of the principles of the theory, defined a particular terminology and constantly applied both of them in his works. The research by Schmitt goes beyond mere theoretical analysis and is largely concerned with problems of both international payments and developing countries, which he examines from his very individual theoretical point of view (Schmitt 1972).

A second set of scholars gathers around Alain Parguez, for many years the editor of the series 'Monnaie et Production', published under his editorship by ISMEA of Paris between 1984 and 1996. The series contains contributions by scholars from various countries. So long as it was published, it was the only really international connection established between French followers of the circulation approach and their counterparts in Anglo-Saxon countries. The group headed by Parguez is strictly connected to French-Canadian authors, among whom the best known are Marc Lavoie and Mario Seccareccia from the University of Ottawa (in fact, one of the first reviews of circuit theory and of the contributions of the main authors belonging to it is due to Lavoie (1987)). The Parguez group is not as particular as Bernard Schmitt in adhering to the conceptual and terminological subtleties on which he often insists, and is largely concerned with present-day problems of economic policy in advanced countries. Among the French and French-Canadian representatives of the circuit theory, Parguez and Lavoie are the two who move closest to the post-Keynesian approach (Parguez 1975 and 1984; Lavoie is himself the author of a handbook titled *Foundations of Post-Keynesian Economic Analysis*, Lavoie 1993).

A third group, active mostly in the 1980s, was formed in Bordeaux around François Poulon. Starting from the basic ideas of circuit theory, Poulon has endeavoured to construct a complete macroeconomic model. Poulon is the only French follower of the theory to have written a complete handbook of macroeconomics (Poulon 1982).

## The circulation approach in Italy

Among the Italian precursors, a special mention is due to Professor Paolo Sylos Labini who, in contrast to the dominant Italian doctrine, has always maintained that the money stock is endogenously determined thanks to the creation of money by the banks in response to the demand for credit from firms (Sylos Labini 1948). In more recent years, the doctrine of the monetary circuit has aroused wide interest among Italian scholars. A detailed analysis of circuit theory is given by Graziani 1989; a typical circuit analysis is performed by Messori 1985.

## The circulation approach in Anglo-Saxon countries

Approaches very similar in content to the circuit approach are to be found in the so-called Anglo-Saxon high theory of the 1930s. An analysis of money circulation identical in substance to the circulation approach is to be found in Keynes's works, in particular in the *Treatise on Money* (1930) as well as in the 1937–39 essays which followed the publication of the

*General Theory* (this point is illustrated in detail in Graziani 1991). A similar approach was followed by Joan Robinson in an often neglected chapter of *The Accumulation of Capital* (Robinson 1956: 25, 'The meaning of money'), as well as by other contemporary Anglo-Saxon authors (Dillard 1980; Godley and Cripps 1981; Godley 1990; Wray 1993; and, along the same lines, Eboli 1991).

## 1.2 Theoretical vicissitudes

Any elementary presentation of monetary theory makes clear that money, besides being a *numéraire* used for measuring prices, performs two main functions: (a) money is an *intermediary of exchange*, since, in present-day economies, payment is nearly always made in money, barter having practically disappeared; (b) *money is a form of wealth*, since anybody can hold the whole or part of his or her own wealth in the form of liquid balances, while waiting to establish what seems to be the most profitable placement.

Money as an intermediary of exchange is the older and more intuitive notion of money. In fact, in the imagination of the person in the street, money is no more than a means of enabling agents to buy commodities. If money, instead of being spent in the market, is kept as an idle balance, this is commonly understood as being a merely temporary destination, connected to the uncertainty of the moment and accepted only by agents waiting to make use of it in its natural function: being exchanged for real goods.

The conception of money as an intermediary of exchange is the first to appear in the history of economic thought. Adam Smith explains how the adoption of money is a consequence of the division of labour and a spontaneous reaction of the market to the practical problems that direct barter would create. After telling the long story of primitive money, Smith concludes: 'It is in this manner that money has become in all civilised nations the universal instrument of commerce, by the intervention of which goods of all kinds are bought and sold, or exchanged for one another' (Smith 1993 [1776], book I, chapter 4: 34). Similarly, in Stuart Mill's words, money is 'the medium through which the incomes of the different members of the community are distributed to them, and the measure by which they estimate their possessions' (Mill 1909 [1848], book III, chapter 7, §3: 487).

If money is a mere intermediary of exchange, and if, as is postulated in general economic equilibrium theory, each agent keeps a strictly balanced budget (equality between the respective values of goods and services bought and sold), the final outcome is that all that an agent buys is paid for by means of real goods or services supplied (this is why supporters of this view insist on the fact that money, if properly understood, while being an intermediary of exchange, is no means of payment in itself). The whole market mechanism appears to be in the nature of a general barter, made easier by the intermediation of money, possibly obscured by the 'veil of money', but not altered in its substance.[4]

Carl Menger, a stauch supporter of the definition of money as an intermediary of exchange, used to consider money as being the spontaneous product of market choices. According to his historical reconstruction of the origin of money, among all goods traded in the market, one of them emerged because of its being scarce, durable and easy to carry.[5] Gradually all

---

[4] Patinkin and Steiger 1989 critically examine the character of the veil assigned to money. Paradoxically, some circuit theorists, like Schmitt and Cencini, come very close to the neoclassical approach in defining money as a mere technical instrument allowing goods to be exchanged on the market. In this view, payments made by an individual are actually completed only when the budget is perfectly balanced so that the purchase of each single commodity has been paid for by means of other commodities. 'Money is a pure instrument of circulation. It is no wealth, nor is it endowed with purchasing power. It is a mere numerical instrument having the function of measuring and making exchange possible' (Cencini and Schmitt 1992: 115).

[5] Menger 1892. Menger's teaching was followed by Hicks, who adds that, as soon as a specific precious metal became a recognised intermediary of exchange, the state was ready to come in and take over the coinage of money (Hicks 1989: 63ff.).

agents came to demand that particular good exclusively as payment for any other goods supplied, with the consequence that that good finally became the general intermediary of all exchanges. In Menger's view, paper money is (and should be) no more than a representative of metal money, this being the only real and sound money.

While being adequate at the intuitive level, the concept of money as a mere intermediary of exchange was abandoned because of two serious analytical problems associated with it, the first being the *correct definition of the utility of money*, the second being the *possibility of considering money itself as an observable magnitude*. Both aspects deserve detailed examination.

The controversy concerning the correct definition of the utility of money, which took place at the end of the nineteenth and the beginning of the twentieth century, was one consequence of the dominance of the theory of value based on utility. At the time, according to the dominant theory, the value of any good was determined by its marginal utility. Money, being used not for direct consumption but as an instrument for acquiring other goods, was not considered to be the source of any direct utility. The utility of money was therefore defined as an indirect utility, determined by the utility of the bundle of commodities that could be purchased by means of a given money stock. This point, already put forward by von Wieser and Böhm-Bawerk, was formulated with special vigour by Maffeo Pantaleoni in his famous *Pure Economics*. When introducing his analysis of money, Pantaleoni writes: '[Money] may be absolutely destitute of all direct utility . . . The more the particular thing we use as money is destitute of direct utility, the more essentially it is money . . . Money is only endowed with an indirect utility, consisting in its power of obtaining for us, solely by means of exchange, some direct commodity' (Pantaleoni 1898: 221). The same principle was finally codified by Ludwig von Mises in his famous 1912 *Theory of Money*: 'In the case of money subjective use-value and subjective exchange-value coincide . . . The subjective value of money always depends on the subjective value of the other economic goods that can be obtained in exchange for it' (von Mises 1934 [1912]: 97, 98).

However, as Helfferich convincingly remarked, the volume of goods that a unit of money can buy depends on the level of money prices and therefore on the exchange value of money. Thus, in order to measure the utility of money and its value, one should already know its value. We are clearly arguing in a circle (Helfferich 1919; a detailed discussion of the same problem is contained in Schumpeter 1954, part IV, chapter 8: 1086–91).

In fact von Mises himself was fully conscious of the problem and, in a somewhat devious way, tried to find a solution to it. Von Mises tried to introduce a distinction, which subsequently entered into common usage, between individual experiments and market experiments (Patinkin 1965, Mathematical Appendix, n. 1). Individuals, when entering the market, ignore the ruling prices. This does not prevent them from preparing a strategy of action (their demand or supply schedule) or from determining the quantities that they are prepared to buy or sell as functions of all possible prices. What consumers decide upon when entering the market is not the quantity that they will actually buy (a quantity that will only be determined once the prevailing price is known), but their demand function, in which prices appear as parameters. In any possible price constellation, money will have a different purchasing power and therefore a different utility. The individual is ready to face any possible set of prices and therefore any possible value of money. Individuals ignore the actual level of prices; but, by considering prices as parameters, they are ready to consider their own money balance as being endowed with a marginal utility which will itself depend on the actually prevailing set of prices. On the basis of plans previously drawn, individuals will start negotiations, thus contributing to the determination of equilibrium prices. Once the set of prices that makes demand and supply equal in each market has been reached, negotiations come to an end, equilibrium prices are known to all participants and the marginal utility of money is also determined. It is a well-known principle of demand theory that the reciprocal interdependence of prices and quantities exchanged does not make the problem indeterminate. In the same way, the interdependence between prices and value of money does not lead to a circular argument.

Unfortunately, von Mises's presentation (1934 [1912]: 97–107) was made obscure by his attempt (this one surely wrong) to demonstrate that a single individual is able to know the utility of money *even before* the market has reached an equilibrium position. In order to show that an individual is able to plan his market strategy before knowing the equilibrium level of prices, von Mises imagines that the individual, when entering the market, assumes present prices to be equal to those prevailing in the previous period. The same prices should determine the value of money, and therefore its utility. Any period thus relates to the previous one, back to an initial time in history when commodity money was used not as money but as a material good having a direct utility. The value of money thus comes to depend on the value of gold as a commodity. Von Mises's initial intuition was correct. But the development of his reasoning was unfortunate and he was himself accused of arguing in a circle (Patinkin 1965, appendix D).

From this moment onwards, the theory of money took a different route. Instead of reformulating von Mises's reasoning in a more correct way, it seemed simpler to modify the theoretical approach at its very root. Thus the idea was introduced that the utility of money is not an indirect one (derived from the utility of goods that money can buy), but the direct utility that an agent draws from having a money holding. By this definition, money is considered to yield utility not when spent but when kept idle. An individual who demands money in order to spend it is considered as demanding goods, not money; a true demand for money is only expressed by individuals wanting money in order to keep it as a liquid balance.

Clear traces of a similar idea can be found in Marshall (1975 [1870]: 166–7) and Wicksell (1936 [1898], chapter 6, section A). The first to give a rigorous analytical formulation of this approach was the almost forgotten economist Karl Schlesinger. In an essay published in 1914 on the *Theory of a Money and Credit Economy* (Schlesinger 1914), he suggested that the need that money satisfies, rather than being a need for real goods that money can buy, is the need of having a liquid balance as protection against uncertainty. In Schlesinger's own words: 'Let us suppose that chance deficits cannot be covered by credits. They can then be covered only by selling the firm . . . or else by cash reserves held against such contingencies . . . The individual loss in not earning an interest on these cash reserves can be regarded as a risk premium' (Schlesinger 1914: 96–7). Schlesinger's book went unnoticed and remained totally ignored for many years.

Indications along similar lines are given by Irving Fisher, who writes: '. . . in a world of chance and sudden changes, quick saleability, or liquidity, is a great advantage . . . The most saleable of all property is, of course, money: and as Karl [*sic*] Menger pointed out, it is precisely this saleability which makes it money. The *convenience* of surely being able, without any previous preparation, to dispose of it for any exchange, in other words its *liquidity*, is itself a sufficient return upon the capital which a man seems to keep idle in money form' (Fisher 1930: 215–16; similar statements are in Fisher 1963 [1911]: 8ff.). Finally J. R. Hicks's famous article of 1933 made it clear that money yields utility in the form of protection against uncertainty, and that consequently the utility of money comes not from spending but rather from *not* spending it. The demand for money is therefore present only in conditions of uncertainty and is a demand for a stock of wealth. This result finally overcame the problems connected to the definition of the utility of money and meant that money could be considered capable of yielding direct utility. Thanks to his rigorous presentation, Hicks was credited as having been the first to resolve the utility-of-money controversy.

The second kind of problem connected to the definition of money as an intermediary of exchange emerges most clearly in the analysis of money circulation in modern times.

Nowadays, money is paper money introduced into the market by means of bank credit. The banking system grants credit to single agents having to make a payment, for instance firms having to hire labour and pay wages. The moment wages are paid, the firms become debtors and the wage earners become creditors of the bank. The result of the operation is the emergence of a stock of money equal in amount to the credit granted to firms. The money stock stays in existence as long as the debt of the firms is not repaid. Once the debt is repaid, the money circuit is closed and the money initially created is also destroyed.

Let us now assume a world free from uncertainty and populated by perfectly rational agents. In this world, any agent will go into debt only at the very moment in which he has to make a payment. Similarly, any agent who receives a money payment tries to spend it as soon as possible on goods or on securities. Both kinds of expenditure bring the money back to the firms, who immediately repay their debt to the bank. In a hypothetical world free from uncertainty and from frictions, the aforementioned steps would take place in an immediate succession with no time lag. This means that money is created, passed on from one agent to the next, and destroyed in the same instant. If this is the case, money is no longer an observable magnitude and the paradoxical result emerges of a monetary economy being defined as an economy in which money, in spite of its being by definition necessary for exchanges to take place, escapes any observation and any possible measurement. If all agents behaved as J.B. Say imagined, namely spending any amount of money as soon as received, the velocity of circulation would be infinite, money would be destroyed as soon as it was created and any attempt to measure the money stock in existence at any given moment of time would invariably produce a zero result. As a paradoxical consequence, the image would emerge of a monetary economy (in the sense of an economy having ruled out barter and in which all payments are regulated in terms of money) in which money did not exist.[6]

A consequence is that it is almost impossible to reconcile a similar definition with the Walrasian model of general equilibrium. If, as is typical of the Walrasian model, the negotiations for the definition of equilibrium prices precede actual exchanges, and if all exchanges take place at the same moment at equilibrium prices, all agents simultaneously sell and buy goods having an identical total value. Thus the whole process of exchanges takes the form of a great barter, which no longer requires the use of money. If the model is extended to a number of periods, but the assumption of predetermined prices is preserved by assuming the presence of future markets, equilibrium prices are simultaneously determined for the current as well as for all future periods. Once more, the model depicts an economy which can work without money. The theoretical approach of the Walrasian model, owing to the simultaneous determination of all present and future prices, ignores any possible uncertainty, thus ruling

---

[6] Knut Wicksell saw this problem and envisaged a model structured so as to avoid it: in Wicksell's model, wage earners buy finished products not from producers but from traders, who sell the product of the previous production cycle and pay the revenue into bank deposits earning the current rate of interest. At the end of the current production cycle, traders buy the finished product and replenish their stock. In this case, an amount of money equal to the initial liquidity requirements of producers is always in existence.

out any possible demand for liquid balances.[7] General equilibrium theory, owing to the problem of reconciling it with the theory of a monetary economy, was downgraded to the theory of barter economy.

For money to be an observable magnitude, it must be kept by single agents for a finite period of time, no matter how short, thus taking the form of a cash balance, be it notes or bank deposits. Since, as mentioned earlier, liquid balances are kept as a protection against uncertainty, this means that, for money to be an observable magnitude, the market must be operating under uncertainty. If we move in a hypothetical market free from uncertainty, liquid balances disappear, and with them the possibility of observing and measuring the money stock in existence. As Benetti and Cartelier have remarked, once one decides to abstract from uncertainty, the very existence of money balances is ruled out, except when the economy is out of equilibrium (Benetti and Cartelier 1990). In fact, when Keynes, in the *General Theory*, defined money as a cash balance having the function of protecting agents from uncertainty, he was choosing the only analytically satisfactory solution and accepting the only possible conception of money which could make it an observable magnitude. It is no surprise that the Keynesian approach to money has been considered for over half a century the final conclusion of a long controversy.

---

[7] A similar result is well known. As long ago as 1930, Erik Lindhal, who was working in the framework of a general equilibrium model, had noticed that money creation on the part of the banking system is only possible out of equilibrium (Lindhal 1930, part II, chapter 1). The same remark can be found in later authors (Debreu 1959; Arrow and Hahn 1972: 338; Hahn 1982). An indirect proof of this point is that Clower, in order to give a role to money in a general equilibrium context, builds a model in which, in contrast to the typical structure of Walrasian models, exchanges are not synchronised and can be started only if at least some of the agents dispose of an initial money balance to finance their initial expenditures (since Clower does not consider bank credit, the nature of money in his model remains undefined; Clower 1969: 202–11. An excellent review of the problem is given by Villieu 1993).

The definition of money as a stock of wealth was considered unobjectionable and became universally accepted.[8] However, once universally adopted, the definition of money as a stock of liquid wealth went through gradual alterations and through a parallel degeneration. Since money was no longer considered in its role as a means of payment and was considered only as a part of the stock of wealth, it was no longer identified with the flow of payments performed over a period of time. A consequence was a tendency to consider the stock of money as a given parameter.

Nothing would have prevented, in principle, money being placed on the same footing as any other commodity, and the production of money being analysed along with the production of other commodities. By proceeding in this direction, it would have been possible to analyse the formation of the money stock as the result of negotiations between banks and firms in the money market. In fact the very definition of equilibrium was an obstacle in this direction. A general equilibrium is defined not only by the objective conditions (equality of supply and demand in all markets), but also by the so-called subjective conditions, requiring that the budget constraint be satisfied for all agents so that all individual budgets are rigorously balanced. The budget constraint being interpreted in its most restrictive meaning (not only as an equality between assets and liabilities but as a strict balance of current income and expenditure), equilibrium was made to coincide with a position in which all agents have

---

[8] An aside is in order. As previously mentioned, Menger emphasised the fact that a specific commodity emerges as money as the consequence of a spontaneous choice made by market agents. In the *Treatise on Money*, Keynes, following Knapp, had defined money as a means of payment recognised by the state: '. . . it is a peculiar characteristic of money contracts that it is the State . . . which decides what it is that must be delivered as a lawful or customary discharge of a contract . . .', Keynes 1971 [1930], vol. 1: 4, 6. In the *General Theory*, while trying to demonstrate that, owing to uncertainty, once money is present it may become the more convenient form of wealth, Keynes doesn't give any explicit definition of money. Knapp's definition has been recently revived in a most convinced way by Wray 1998.

extinguished any possible debt, including their debt to the banking sector. If in equilibrium all debts have been extinguished, the money stock has disappeared. Once more it seems impossible to reconcile a rigorously defined equilibrium position with the presence of money, with the only difference that, in this case, the disappearance of money does not depend on an inconsistency between a demand for money balances and rational behaviour in the absence of uncertainty, but on the simple fact that agents automatically eliminate the presence of money by simply respecting their own budget constraints (on this point more will be added later, see §2.2).

This time, the way out was found by enlarging the model and including in it the government sector. In principle, the government sector is not held to have a balanced budget. Consequently, the presence of a current deficit in the government's budget is not incompatible with a general equilibrium. More precisely, a position of full equilibrium is defined as one in which the amount of government debt not financed by placement of securities (and therefore the amount of legal money outstanding) is equal to the amount of money demanded in the market. In fact nowadays this kind of solution (money entirely created by the government deficit and being in the nature of an exogenous magnitude) is presented as an obvious truth in any introductory presentation.

However, this solution is in itself weak. To begin with, it modifies the very nature of fiscal policy in that the level of the government deficit is conceived as determined not by the requirements of the community in terms of government services, but by the money stock needed to ensure the smooth circulation of goods in the market. The government is no longer viewed as a supplier of social services but as a supplier of liquidity (Riese 1998: 56). If both roles of the government are to be satisfied at the same time, the final level of government deficit has to be such as to fund the provision of social services while at the same time supplying the required stock of money – two targets hard to reach with the same level of government deficit (Sawyer 1985: 16; Tobin 1986: 11).

In addition to that, if, as is customary in most of modern macroeconomics, monetary theory considers money as a given stock, this leaves unexplained how the available purchasing power is distributed among single agents or among social groups present in the market. This is no great loss for anyone who is a true follower of neoclassical theory. In fact, in a neoclassical theoretical perspective the purchasing power at the disposal of each individual does not depend on the money stock in his possession but on the amount of real goods or services that he is willing to supply and able to sell. The initial distribution of the money stock among single agents, in itself, is not a relevant factor. The same is no great loss either to the followers of the post-Keynesian school, especially to the followers of Kaldor. To them, the banking system performs a totally passive role vis-à-vis the demand for credit coming from producers. The firms can consequently carry out their production plans free from any financial constraint.

The same loss becomes, however, a substantial limitation to anyone who thinks that, when creating liquidity, the banking system operates a selection process. In this case, the agents endowed with an autonomous and potentially unlimited purchasing power are not all possible agents present in the market but only those who are considered eligible for bank credit. These usually belong to the class of entrepreneurs, to the exclusion of wage earners. Circuit theorists subscribe to this train of thought (this point is dealt with later on in this chapter, §1.4). To them, the definition of money as a means of payment remains an essential element in the analysis of macroeconomic equilibrium.

## 1.3  The circuit version

In opposition to the dominant Keynesian view of money as a stock of wealth, circuit theorists remark that the first and foremost role of money is to make possible the circulation of commodities. Therefore money appears in its authentic capacity only when a good is exchanged against money and money passes from the balances of one agent to the balances of some other one. In this perspective, the more rigorous among circuit theorists insist on the fact that when money is kept idle, even if only to cover future payments, it is no longer an instrument of circulation but rather a stock of wealth (Schmitt 1996: 132ff.).

In opposition also to the neoclassical view of money as a mere intermediary of exchange, circuit theorists emphasise the fact that money should be viewed as an authentic means of payment. Money, they remark, enters the market by way of bank credit. When a firm is making use of a bank overdraft, it is in fact acquiring commodities or labour without giving any real good in exchange; which means that it is using money as a means of payment. In terms of substance, circuit theorists remark that money exerts its primary influence on macroeconomic equilibrium when it is used for buying commodities and not when it is kept as an idle balance. Under this aspect, circuit theorists clearly differ from the followers of Keynes, who insist on the fact that money makes its presence felt just because it can be kept as a liquid balance and become idle money.

The decision of circuit theorists to shift their attention away from the time that liquid balances are kept as such and to concentrate on the time that money is used in order to make a payment displaces the focus of theoretical analysis. The dominant theory of money, when analysing the demand for money, enquires about its motivations and possible fluctuations; when analysing the money supply, the theory often considers the money stock as the result of independent decisions taken by the monetary authorities. Circuit theorists instead concentrate their analysis on the chain of payments, starting with the initial creation of liquid means, going on to the successive utilisations of money in the market, and ending with the final destruction of money. The very term 'monetary circuit' draws its origin from the fact that the theory examines the complete life cycle of money, from its creation by the banking system, through its circulation in the market, to its being repaid to the banks and consequent destruction.

## 1.4   Circuit theories and neoclassical analysis

The approach adopted by circuit theorists opens a deep theoretical cleavage separating the circuit doctrine both from neoclassical and from Keynesian theory.

It is a well-known fact that neoclassical theory has been the object of a number of analytical criticisms: starting with the older objections from students of welfare theory (lack of perfect competition, external economies or diseconomies, increasing or constant returns, presence of indivisibilities), down to Sraffa's critique concerning the possibility of measuring capital and therefore of applying the marginal theory of distribution, and on to the modern theories of asymmetrical information and of interdependence between quality and price.

Most if not all of these criticisms do not reject the individualistic approach typical of neoclassical theory. On the contrary, according to circuit theorists, so long as this approach is preserved, the fundamental limits of neoclassical theory are not overcome. The first and most important of those limits, according to circuit theorists, is that any theory based on an individualistic approach is necessarily confined to microeconomics and is unable to build a true macroeconomic analysis. A proof of that is given by the fact that all theories based on an individualistic approach have in common the definition of macroeconomics as the result of an aggregation performed on a microeconomic model and not as an independent analysis based on new and different assumptions.

In the perspective of circuit theory, a simple aggregation of the individual behaviour functions doesn't turn a microeconomic model into a true macroeconomic theory. The starting point for a construction of a macroeconomic model can only be the identification of the social groups present in the community, followed by the definition of the conditions necessary for their reproduction and perpetuation over time. An example of a true macroeconomic approach is given by the classical economists, who started from an *a priori* subdivision of society into a number of social classes, each of them having a different initial wealth endowment (landowners own productive resources, entrepreneurs are able to organise productive factors, wage earners can only supply their own labour). The same can be said of Marxian analysis, based on the distinction between capitalists and proletarians, a distinction corresponding to the separation between labour and means of production. The same is also true of Keynes, who made use of a sort of *a priori* distinction between consumers, who evaluate consumption goods according to their immediate utility, and investors, who evaluate capital goods according to subjective and uncertain profit expectations.

In a similar perspective, circuit theorists introduce a preliminary distinction between producers and wage earners, producers having access to bank credit and wage earners being excluded from it. The two groups enter the market having different initial endowments. Entrepreneurs, being admitted to bank credit, can rely on a potentially unlimited purchasing power, while wage earners can only dispose of as much money as they have previously earned. The two social groups have to comply with totally different budget constraints, which makes a basic difference in the definition of their own behaviours.

The contrast with neoclassical theory appears even more clearly if one thinks of the fact that in a perfect market, such as the one assumed in the neoclassical model, the fact of having money actually available does not create a constraint to the purchasing power of the agent. As already mentioned, in the neoclassical model, while it is true that no agent can violate his own budget constraint, the purchasing power of each individual is determined by magnitudes which are not monetary but real in nature, such as his working ability and the amount of his real fortune. In a perfect market, any real resource can be converted into money at the ruling price, whenever the opportunity arises to exchange it for a different good. In this setting any possible liquid balance is but one of the various kinds of wealth pertaining to the agent and deriving from real income previously produced. Even more: any agent expecting to get in the future a higher flow of income, or to become the owner of new wealth, has access to bank credit and can get immediate liquid resources against the promise to repay the debt when due. Therefore, the purchasing power of an agent is not limited by his present wealth but is determined by his ability to produce real goods in a much wider time horizon.

Circuit theorists start with a totally opposite vision. In their view, in a monetary economy, precise mechanisms prevail which bring purchasing power into the hands of some agents rather than others. To begin with, since the market does not guarantee full employment, the purchasing power of an agent is never determined by the simple ability to perform productive work but rather by the fact of being actually employed and of being paid in terms of money. The same is true of credit, which is not granted to anyone presumably able to repay his debt, but only to selected agents, usually being productive firms. Only firms have actual access to bank credit and therefore enjoy a purchasing power exceeding their present wealth. As a rule, instead, wage earners can enter the market only after they have sold their own labour and received the corresponding pay.[9] A similar assumption clearly echoes the

---

[9] Such an assumption is explicitly made by Benetti and Cartelier (1990) and by Cartelier (1996). This is by no means a new idea. In the eighteenth century it was commonly accepted that money and power should go hand in hand (a most persuasive analysis of this point is performed by Giacomin 1994). In some sense the same assumption is to be found

Marxian distinction between a class of property owners and a class of propertyless workers, a distinction now turned into the division between a class able to spend beyond its current income and another class that is subject to a budget constraint determined by already earned income. Once this assumption is accepted, the theorem of the neutrality of money is clearly rejected in point of principle, since any creation of money increases the spending ability of a well-defined group of agents, which means that the effects it exerts on the price level cannot be neutral.[10]

Similarly, circuit theory parts company with the neoclassical approach in the definition of the money stock. Neoclassical theory concentrates on the equilibrium position which is reached when the stock of money equals the liquid balances permanently required by the public. Circuit theory tries instead to consider the whole life cycle of money, starting with its creation by means of bank loans and ending with its destruction when those loans are repaid. In a traditional setting, based on agricultural production, money can be considered as being created at the beginning of the production cycle and gradually destroyed as bank loans are repaid. In this case the average money stock would equal half of the initial finance. In a modern setting, where synchronised industrial

in Marxian thought. Marx defines a capitalist as an agent having the property of means of production and being adequately endowed with money. Access to bank credit assures precisely the necessary endowment of liquidity. Nowadays this is no longer a common assumption. More often than not, contemporary literature insists on the fact that credit granted to households equals or even exeeds credit granted to firms (a well-documented argument is contained in Howells 2001). It is however highly debatable whether credit granted to households is really given to consumers or rather is in fact indirectly granted to firms, by allowing consumers to buy finished products.

[10] Schumpeter, when discussing the traditional principle according to which money is just a veil that can and must be removed whenever the analysis concerns 'the fundamental features of the economic process, just as a veil must be drawn aside if we are to see the face behind it', warns the reader that 'the essential features of the capitalist process may depend upon the veil and that the face behind it is incomplete without it' (Schumpeter 1954, chapter 6: 277, 278).

production is the rule, loans are continually granted and continually repaid. In a stationary economy, the money stock would be equal to the amount of initial finance created by the banks.

## 1.5  Circuit theory and Keynesian analysis

The very fact of considering the unequal initial distribution of purchasing power creates a conflict between circuit theorists and the Keynesian school. It has already been recalled that the Keynesian school gives a special weight to money only because money can be kept as an idle balance. In fact, in Keynesian models, sudden shifts in the speculative demand for money are responsible for demand failures and for both recurrent and prolonged unemployment crises. To circuit theorists, on the other hand, fluctuations in liquidity preference and in aggregate demand, while being an indisputable element of historical experience, are not the most relevant aspect of a market economy. The path of an economy is influenced in a much deeper way by money and credit flows, by the investment decisions emerging from the negotiations between banks and firms, by the proportions in which aggregate production is divided between consumption and investment goods, and by the consequent distribution of national income between wages and profits. These are the basic mechanisms explaining, among other things, fluctuations in aggregate demand, the same fluctuations that the Keynesian school traces back to the simple action of liquidity preference.

Today's macroeconomic theory, while originating from Keynes's *General Theory*, is usually presented in the form of the IS–LM model, a version due to Hicks, Hansen and Modigliani. The IS–LM model is rejected by circuit theorists on the ground that, by considering the money stock as a given magnitude, it omits the analysis of the creation of money, neglects the relationships between banks and firms (in the Hicks–Hansen model, banks and firms are in fact aggregated into one single sector), and consequently ignores the interdependence between the IS and the LM lines. Not all of these criticisms are raised against Keynes's original model as expressed in the *General Theory*; yet, circuit theorists make no secret of the fact that, between the two main Keynesian works, they assign a clear preference to the *Treatise on Money* over the *General Theory*.

## 1.6 Circuit theory and post-Keynesian theory

On one single point another divergence emerges between circuit theorists and the post-Keynesian school. It is a well-known fact that the post-Keynesians of the first generation (Nicholas Kaldor, Joan Robinson, Richard Kahn) do not consider as relevant the problem of the money supply, a problem that circuit theorists consider to be a fundamental one. Justification by the post-Keynesians for neglecting the money supply is grounded on two main arguments. The first is that, since the monetary authorities are forced to satisfy the demand for liquidity coming from the market, the money supply tends to be infinitely elastic. The second argument is that, even if the monetary authorities could limit the amount of credit being granted by the banks, the market would find other forms of liquidity, mainly consisting in credit mutually granted by single agents. This would allow the agents to carry out their own production plans whatever the credit policy run by the monetary authorities. The conclusion drawn by post-Keynesians is that liquidity is never a serious constraint.[11]

A consequence of a similar approach is that post-Keynesians never analyse the relationships between banks and firms. Here a clear divergence emerges between the post-Keynesian and the circuit schools. The relationships between

---

[11] Kaldor 1985; Leijonhufvud and Heymann 1991. Keynes himself expressed a totally different idea: '. . . the investment market can become congested through shortage of cash. It can never become congested through shortage of saving' (Keynes 1973c [1937]: 669 [222]).

firms and banks are fundamental to circuit theoreticians, since such relationships determine the amount of liquidity available. Under this aspect, smaller divergences emerge between the circuit doctrine and the second generation of post-Keynesians (as represented by S. Weintraub, P. Davidson, H.P. Minsky, J. Kregel, and B.J. Moore), who pay instead great attention to the problems concerning the money supply and the finance available to firms.

A point of convergence between circuit theory and the post-Keynesian school can be found in the analysis of income distribution. Here circuit theorists follow closely what was once named the Keynes–Kalecki formulation. First sketched by D.H. Robertson (1926) and by Keynes in his *Treatise on Money* (Keynes 1971 [1930]), this approach to income distribution was developed by Kalecki (1991 [1942]), Kaldor (1956), and Joan Robinson (1956). According to this approach, firms can decide the activity levels and the nature of production (consumption or investment goods), while wage earners, whatever the level of their money wage, can only buy real consumer goods in the amount made available by producers (Kregel 1973, chapter 10). Therefore the actual level of real wages is determined by producers and not by regular market negotiations. At most it can be the object of a political conflict. This point, emphasising the widely different market power of producers and wage earners, is sometimes expressed by saying that, in the labour market, wage earners can only negotiate money wages, never real wages. This doesn't depend on wage earners being irrational agents, or on their being subject to money illusion. It is instead a typical feature of any market economy that producers can decide the proportions of consumer goods and investment goods produced, while wage earners can only decide how their money wages will be spent. If wage earners could actually negotiate the level of real wages, producers would correspondingly lose the power to determine the level and the nature of production. Assuming that producers can control the real side of production is tantamount to assuming that wage earners can only negotiate the money level of wages. As François Simiand once said, 'the level of money wages is a fact; the level of real wages is an opinion' (Simiand 1932, vol. 1: 160).

It is worth noting that the same mechanism indicated by Keynes and Kalecki for income distribution within the private sector is admitted by the neoclassical theory for the distribution of income between the private and the government sectors. This is the mechanism of the so-called inflation tax, by which the government sector, without applying any explicit tax, gets hold of a portion of national product (on this point more will be added in chapter 2, §2.5). There is however a difference in that, according to neoclassical theory, the ability to get hold of real goods by using purely monetary instruments is strictly limited to the government sector, and the mechanism making this possible is considered a wholly negative deviation from the ideal working of a market system. In the Keynes–Kalecki formulation, the same mechanism is viewed instead as the normal working of a market economy and is considered to work in favour of profits.

## 1.7 The basic ideas of the theory of the monetary circuit

The ideas lying at the basis of the theory of the monetary circuit can be summarised in the following propositions:

a)  Money is in the nature of credit money and in modern times is represented by bank credit.
b)  Credit money is created whenever an agent spends money granted to him by a bank and is destroyed whenever a bank credit is repaid.
c)  Money being produced and introduced into the market by means of negotiations between banks and firms is an endogenous variable.

d)    The community is divided into two different groups of agents. The first, represented by producers, has access to bank credit and as a consequence enjoys a purchasing power which is not constrained by the level of real income or by ownership of real wealth. The second group, represented by wage earners, can only spend already-earned income.

e)    Since agents are not granted credit on the same footing, the system of relative prices reflects the way in which purchasing power has been granted to different agents. As a consequence, money is never neutral.

f)    A complete theoretical analysis has to explain the whole itinerary followed by money, starting with the moment credit is granted, going through the circulation of money in the market, and reaching the final repayment of the initial bank loan. Money being created by the banking sector and being extinguished when it goes back to the same sector, its existence and operation can be described as a circuit.

g)    Since macroeconomic analysis explains how the creation of money determines both the division of production between consumption and investment goods and the distribution of income between wages and profits, it also shows that the role of money goes far beyond that of making exchanges easier or improving the technical working of the market. To the social group being admitted to bank credit, money is, at the economic level, a source of profits and, at the social level, a source of power.

## 1.8  A synthetic description of the monetary circuit

The different phases of the monetary circuit can be easily described. In this first synthetic representation, only four agents are considered: the central bank, commercial banks, firms, and wage earners. The government sector will be introduced later on.[12]

*Step one*: A decision is taken by the banks to grant credit to firms, thus enabling them to start a process of production. The amount of credit supplied by the banks at this stage can be denominated *initial finance*.[13] As already mentioned, circuit theorists usually assume that only firms are admitted to bank credit.

If we consider firms as one integrated and consolidated sector, the only purchase firms have to make before starting production is to hire labour, and their only payment is the wage bill. All other exchanges can be neglected, being internal to the firms sector. Therefore the demand for bank credit coming from producers depends only on the wage rate and on the number of workers that firms intend to hire (Moore 1983, 1984; Graziani 1984).

It is clear that if, instead of considering firms as a whole, we were considering a single isolated firm, the situation would be different. A single firm has to cover not only the wage bill but other current costs, including possible purchases of durable goods, such as machinery and other forms of investment. Still the simplified aggregate representation by no means alters the substance of the picture. Let us consider the case of a single firm having been granted credit for the

---

[12] A similar description can be found in Wicksell 1936 [1898], chapter 9, section B. Going back in the past, a remarkable description of the circulation of money is given by Galiani. His is not a commodity money but an immaterial fiat money, very similar to Wicksell's pure credit (Galiani 1780, book II, chapter 1). In more recent times, the same description can be found in Parguez 1981; Lavoie 1987, 1993: 151–69, and 1996; Graziani 1989; Wray 1996. It is debatable whether the description of the circulation of money as a monetary circuit is implicitly present in Keynes's thought. In favour of this interpretation: Barrère 1979: 160, 1988a: 22; Poulon 1982, chapter 11: 300; Graziani 1987, 1989; against it Kregel 1986b.

[13] This step was analysed by Keynes when introducing his 'finance motive for holding money', an innovation which gave rise to a long debate (Graziani 1984). Cesaroni (2001) puts forward a number of remarks critical of Keynes's construction.

construction of a plant. As soon as the firm starts operating, the liquidity is passed on to the firms employed in the construction, who pass it on to their own employees. Thus, albeit in an indirect way, the credit initially granted is totally turned into wages. At the end of the process, the firm being granted the initial credit is in debt to the banking system, while wage earners are creditors of the banks: exactly as though the firm had itself carried out the construction for which the credit had been initially granted. We can therefore conclude that considering firms as one integrated sector simplifies the reasoning without altering its substance.

Since the payment of the wage bill is followed by the production of some kind of finished or semi-finished product, there is a correspondence between the wage bill paid and the cost of produced commodities. The initial requirement of bank credit can therefore be measured both by the amount of the wage bill and by the value of inventories in possession of the firms. Some authors in fact prefer to say that the credit requirements of the firms are measured by the money cost of commodities being produced (this is the definition initially given by Hawtrey (1923), and later on adopted by Godley and Cripps (1981)). To some extent the two definitions are equivalent. If we refer to the bank debt of the firms in a single instant of time, it is correct to set it equal to the money value of commodities produced and not yet sold, namely semi-finished products plus inventories. If we refer to the initial credit requirement of the firms, and therefore to their demand for bank credit, it seems more correct to make credit requirements equal to the wage bill corresponding to the planned level of production.

The last definition has the advantage of bringing to light the clear correspondence existing between the credit market and the labour market. Any increase in money wages or in employment gives rise to a higher credit requirement and to a consequent renegotiation of the agreements between banks and firms. This explains why firms, when negotiating with unions for the determination of money wages, always try to predict the possible reactions of the banking system, since such reactions will finally determine whether or not the agreed wage rates can be paid. The wage policy of the firms thus ultimately depends on the credit policy of the banks.[14]

Negotiations between banks and firms determine the amount of credit and the level of the interest rate.

*Step two*: The second phase of the economic process consists in the decisions concerning production and expenditure. A basic assumption of circuit theory is that firms enjoy total independence when deciding upon the real aspects of production, namely employment levels and the amount of consumer goods and investment goods produced. Wage earners can only take decisions on how to distribute their money incomes between consumption expenditure, addition to cash balances (bank deposits or notes) or purchase of securities (in the present simplified presentation, since we are neglecting the government sector, securities can only be issued by producers).[15]

*Step three*: In the third phase, commodities produced are put on sale. Consumer goods are sold to wage earners, while investment goods are exchanged inside the firms sector (firms having produced means of production sell them to firms making use of them).

The money that wage earners spend in the commodities market, as well as money spent in the financial market on the purchase of securities, flows back to the firms, who can use it to repay their bank debt. To the extent that bank debts are

---

[14] Some authors perform an analysis of the supply curve of the single bank (Messori 1988; Screpanti 1993: 134ff.). Stiglitz (1999) concentrates on the analysis of the behaviour of the banks under asymmetrical information. This aspect will be omitted in the present analysis.

[15] As already mentioned, the image used in circuit theory of an economic mechanism in which firms decide upon the real magnitudes while wage earners can only determine their own monetary expenditures is borrowed from Keynes's *Treatise on Money*; Keynes 1971 [1930], chapters 10 (i): 136, and 20: 315–17; also Keynes 1973c [1937]).

repaid, an equal amount of money is destroyed. To the extent instead that wage earners use their money to increase their own cash balances, an equal amount of money remains in existence in the form of firms' debt and wage earners' credit towards the banks.

*Step four*: Once the initial bank debt is repaid and the money is destroyed, the monetary circuit is closed. New money will be created when the banks grant new credit for a new production cycle. This can take place almost automatically if firms, instead of repaying their bank debt, use the receipts from the sale of commodities and from the placement of securities to begin a new production cycle. In this case, as Keynes remarked, bank credit becomes a sort of 'revolving fund' of constant amount.[16] However, this doesn't mean that the firms have become financially independent: the very fact that they are allowed by the banks to make use of liquidity granted for a previous production cycle implies a renewal of credit on the part of the banks. This can by no means be taken for granted and in fact is tantamount to getting new finance from the banks.

If wage earners spend their incomes entirely – whether on the commodity market or on the financial market – firms will get back the whole of their monetary advances and will be able to repay the whole principal of their bank debt. In this case, as some would say, the circuit is closed 'without losses'. If instead wage earners decide to keep a portion of their savings in the form of liquid balances, firms are unable to repay their bank debt by the same amount. As a consequence, at the end of the production cycle the money initially created will not be entirely destroyed. If banks are now intending to finance a new production cycle equal to the preceding one

---

[16] Keynes 1973b [1937]: 209 [247]. The inverse is also true, namely that a constant supply of credit is necessary to ensure a constant level of production. The last formulation points out the fact that, as remarked a long time ago by F. Machlup, circulating capital is in fact only a different form of fixed capital (Machlup 1932).

by granting the same finance, the total money stock will be increased: precisely, it will be equal to the wage bill plus the new liquid balances set aside by wage earners at the end of the previous cycle.

*Step five*: So far, the above description has omitted the problem of the payment of interest to the banks. It is self-evident that since the only money existing in the market is the money that banks have lent to the firms, even in the most favourable case, the firms can only repay in money the principal of their debt and are anyhow unable to pay interest. In order to get the money needed to satisfy their interest payments, the only thing they can do is to sell part of their product to the banks, which is tantamount to saying that interest can only be paid in kind. A parallel solution, not widely different in substance, is reached if the banks buy equities issued by the firms.[17] The presence of a government sector would not make things easier. A government deficit might bring to the firms the money necessary to pay interest to the banks; but a government debt towards the central bank would remain pending. There seems to be no way out: either a debt equal to the interest payments remains unsatisfied, or interest is paid in kind.

A similar solution, in spite of its being more reasonable, is rejected by more than one author on the ground that it 'ignores the desire to accumulate wealth in monetary form, which is the object of all accumulation in a monetary economy' (Wray 1996: 452). It is indisputable that the banks, like any other entrepreneur, may want to earn profits in money form. But this is only a transient form, while the final destination of money is to be spent in order to make a profitable investment.

## 1.9   A final remark

A conclusion to be drawn from the preceding analysis is that in a closed economy there is only one circumstance which

---

[17] A similar solution is suggested by Bossone 2001: 869, 873.

can produce losses to firms as a whole, and this is the decision of savers to hoard part of their savings in the form of cash balances. It might seem that in an open economy the decision of savers to place part of their savings on the foreign market might be an additional source of losses to national firms as a whole. In fact, in an integrated financial market, national firms might issue securities not only on the national market but also on the financial markets of other countries, thus capturing the liquidity that the decisions of savers might take away from them.

Therefore, if we abstract from the case of an increase in liquidity preference, firms as a whole run no risk of global financial losses. On the other hand, since it cannot be ruled out that single firms may incur losses, this means that, always abstracting from increases in liquidity preference, any loss incurred by a single firm must be balanced by an identical profit earned by some other firm. Mistakes in management made by one single firm, far from making the firms sector weaker, produce higher profits for other firms. This conclusion leads to a careful revisitation of the idea that in a market economy profit can be taken to be an indicator of efficiency. To begin with, the fact that firms as a whole don't make losses is no sign of efficiency, since firms as a whole will always have balanced budgets, whatever their ability to reduce costs or meet consumer preferences. On the other hand, if we consider each single firm separately, the fact that one single firm is making profits is no sign of an especially efficient management, since profits earned by one firm may simply be the mirror image of inefficiencies and consequent losses incurred by other firms.

# 2

# Neoclassical monetary theory

## 2.1  Introduction

One of the main theoretical conclusions of the neoclassical theory of money is that, in a totally frictionless and perfectly competitive market, money performs a wholly neutral role. While allowing exchanges to take place in a more efficient and rational way, and while avoiding the inconveniences of a barter economy, it alters in no way the final equilibrium position (Tobin 1992: 775). As we know, this would only be true if all prices without exception could move at exactly the same speed and in the same proportion – something which would leave relative prices unchanged. Experience shows instead that the reaction of money prices is different in speed and measure, which means that, at least for a while, any inflationary movement brings about an alteration in relative prices. As a consequence, market prices will no longer be equilibrium prices and distortions in the allocation of resources will appear.

The monetary theory of the neoclassical school tries in fact to show that, if we compare a barter economy and a monetary economy (available resources and individual preferences being the same), quantities produced and relative prices are the same. If this is true, money as a result becomes perfectly neutral, a mere veil, as already mentioned, hiding but not changing the substance of the equilibrium position (§1.2). The veil consists in the fact that in a monetary economy prices are no longer quoted in terms of a commodity chosen as *numéraire* but in terms of money. Since, provided that relative prices are unchanged, the level of money prices is wholly irrelevant, moving from a barter to a monetary economy only makes the market more efficient without modifying the results of negotiations.

The relevance of the neoclassical conclusion is strictly connected to the fundamental theorem of welfare economics, according to which, in a fully competitive market, the equilibrium position coincides with an optimal allocation of productive resources. By optimal allocation neoclassical theorists mean that the set of technologies applied and the set of commodities produced allows, within the constraints set by available resources, the highest satisfaction of consumers' preferences.

While neutrality of money is the main theoretical thesis of neoclassical monetary theory, price stability is its main policy recommendation.

## 2.2 Money in the neoclassical school: truism and theory

The principles of the neoclassical school are usually presented in a trivial form, unobjectionable in itself, but having a merely definitional content.

The principle of neutrality is expressed by saying that, if the money stock is an exogenous variable (determined by the monetary authorities), and the quantities of commodities available in the market are given, any variation in the quantity of money in circulation realised by means of an equiproportional variation in the liquid balances held by each single agent produces a proportional variation in all money prices, relative prices and quantities produced remaining unchanged.

A few words are in order to explain why the neoclassical school assumes the money stock to be an exogenous variable.

Of course, any variable can be assumed to be given from outside merely by way of simplification. But in the neoclassical model the assumption of a given money stock may have a deeper analytical justification.

In a position of full equilibrium, equality between demand and supply prevails in all markets and the budget constraints of each single agent are satisfied, which means that, at the end of the chosen period, all debts have been repaid. If, along with other debts, bank debts have also been fully repaid, each loan initially granted by the banks has been extinguished and bank money has been totally destroyed.[1] If an amount of bank deposits is still in existence, this means that at least one agent has a debt pending with at least one bank. In the neoclassical model the government is the only agent allowed, also in an equilibrium position, to be indebted to one bank, the central bank. Therefore, in equilibrium, the only money in existence is money created through the government channel, namely by way of a loan granted to the government by the central bank. This is the meaning of the usual identity defining the money stock typical of all neoclassical models:

$$M_{(t)} = M_{(t-1)} + G - T - (B_{G(t)} - B_{G(t-1)}),$$

where $M$ is the money stock, $G$ is government expenditure, $T$ the tax yield and $B_G$ is the stock of government bonds.

Since it is assumed that in equilibrium agents want to keep a positive money balance, the creation of money in the amount required by the market, far from being a kind of seigniorage, is no more than a fair exchange of real goods (acquired by the government sector) against a different kind of commodity yielding utility to single agents (real balances). If the only stock of money existing in equilibrium is supplied by government expenditure, it becomes legitimate to view it as an exogenous magnitude determined by the monetary authorities. The role of the government deficit thus becomes

---

[1] As De Viti De Marco would say, the only role of money is to ensure perfect compensation between the value of what is brought to the market and the value of what is taken out of it (De Viti De Marco 1990 [1934]: 23ff.).

one of providing money to the market (as already remarked in §1.2, this might give rise to some analytical problems: Tobin 1986: 11; Riese 1998: 57ff.).[2] If the quantities of commodities, the existing money stock and the velocity of circulation are all considered as given magnitudes, the inevitable conclusion is that the general price level, $P$, varies in the same proportion as the quantity of money and that the stability of money prices depends on the stability of the money stock or on the equiproportional increase in $M$ and $Q$. Hence the traditional prescription concerning the stability of money prices: for stable money prices to prevail, the money stock should be stable or increase at the same rate as the amount of commodities exchanged on the market, a result synthesised in the famous identity: $PQ = MV$ first put forward by Irving Fisher (1963 [1911]: 24–8).

Similar results are often criticised as clear truisms. It is in fact self-evident that if the increase in the quantity of money takes place by way of an equiproportional increase in the cash balances of each single agent, the distribution of real wealth is unchanged. The consequent equiproportional increase in all prices leaves the real income of each agent unchanged. If the distribution of both real wealth and real income is unaltered, relative prices will also be unchanged.

However, a similar interpretation doesn't do full justice to the neoclassical school, a school that has always made an effort to keep its results far above the mere tautological level. A correct formulation of the two principles of neutrality and stability cannot be made to descend from *ad hoc* assumptions

---

[2] It should, however, be remembered that the most serious and rigorous supporters of the quantity theory of money, such as Wicksell, von Mises, and Hayek, refused to consider the money stock as a given magnitude, the amount of which the monetary authorities can vary at will. They all considered instead the existing money stock as originating from bank credit. In their models, the money stock is therefore an endogenous variable. What they tried to do was to ascertain the conditions for price stability and neutrality of money to be valid in a model endowed with endogenous mechanisms for the creation of money.

specially introduced for the purpose of demonstrating the properties of money. Both principles should depend on the same assumptions on which the general theory of prices is based.

The basic assumptions of the neoclassical model can be expressed by three main propositions:

a) *A behavioural assumption*: each individual is endowed with a set of personal and fully independent preferences.

b) *A technological assumption*: each individual knows the technologies allowing the transformation of productive resources into finished products.

c) *An institutional assumption*: perfect competition prevails in each single market, where all agents rigorously observe their budget constraint.

When dealing with a monetary economy, the definition of the budget constraint requires some clarification. If the budget constraint has to be satisfied at each single instant, this means that each agent simultaneously buys and sells commodities having the same market value. In this case, the substance of the economy is more in the nature of a barter even if working as a monetary economy. The same would be true if a commodity money is used, for instance a gold money having equal intrinsic and market value. In this case, the budget constraint of each single agent would necessarily be satisfied at each single instant. This is why many traditional thinkers believe that a commodity money is the only true money: to them, as Keynes once said, the preference for a metallic currency, or for a fully convertible paper money, is a sort of moral principle, essential for exchanges to be really fair (Keynes 1983 [1914]).

If the budget constraint in its looser formulation is accepted, money, being in the form of cash balances, appears as an observable variable within each single period and disappears only when the final position of full equilibrium is reached. It can be said that money, as Benetti and Cartelier (1990) have emphasised, performs the role of financing temporary disequilibria in the budgets of single agents. On the other hand, provided that the budget constraint of each agent is finally satisfied, individual behaviour is not altered by the presence of temporary debt and credit positions and consequently the final equilibrium position is not modified either (Tobin 1980).

## 2.3   The equality between savings and investment

In the equilibrium position, demand should equal supply in all markets. Since in a macroeconomic model only two commodities are assumed to be present (consumption goods and investment goods), if one of the two markets is in equilibrium the other must be in equilibrium too. The general equilibrium condition for the commodities market is therefore just one, namely the equality between savings and investment. The way in which such equality is described in terms of demand and supply deserves some attention.

Walras knew all too well that while on the supply side a number of different investment goods are produced, on the demand side savers express a general demand for a commodity yielding the maximum possible return. Walras therefore introduced a general market, where an imaginary commodity denominated *e* (the initial of the French *excédent*, or the excess of income over consumption) is sold by savers and bought by investors (Walras 1954 [1926], lesson 23, n. 240). As we shall see in what follows, followers of the circulation approach adopt a different solution, at the same time clearer and more adherent to reality, consisting in the introduction of a market for securities. In this market, producers sell securities to savers wishing to place their savings and earn a return.

None of these solutions is followed by the neoclassical school. In the neoclassical model, the equality between savings and investment is reached thanks to the action of the banks. This is one of the most delicate and debatable aspects of the neoclassical model.

In order to fully understand the problems raised by the neoclassical formulation of a monetary equilibrium, it should be recalled that a clear difference exists between the classical school (Smith, Ricardo, Malthus) on one side and the neoclassical authors on the other in an apparently remote field of economic theory, namely *the theory of wages*.

The classical school considers real wages as being rigorously *paid in advance*. Even if wages are usually paid after the corresponding labour has been supplied (for instance, at the end of the week, or month, or after the delivery of commodities), this does not mean that they are paid after the production period has been completed. The assumption of the classical school was in fact that wages are paid *before* the finished product has been completed. A similar assumption is connected to the fact that classical authors had in mind agriculture as the typical sector of production, a sector where wage earners would be waiting for a whole year before getting their means of subsistence, which is clearly impossible. The same assumption of real wages being paid in advance might also be connected to reasons of image. If wages are paid in advance, they are paid from the output of the previous period, i.e. from the capitalists' savings, which can be seen as the source of the famous and debated 'wage fund'. The level of the wage fund, clearly depending on the level of output in the previous period and on the propensity to save of capitalists, determines the wage bill of the current period. Now a world in which capitalists limit their own personal consumption in order to give employment to workers yields the image of an equitable world in which profits appear as the well-deserved remuneration for forgone consumption.

A similar image of the production process lies at the basis of the definition of investment given by the classical school. In the classical model, where real wages are paid in advance, investment is not defined as the amount of newly produced capital goods (this was to be the definition adopted by the neoclassical school). Classical economists instead define investment as the amount of resources engaged in current production. If we consider capitalists as a class, total investment equals the wage bill (if we consider also landowners, investment will be the sum total of the wage bill and of the rent paid to landowners, since what capitalists invest in production is given by their outlays in favour of any member of a different class). If we neglect landowners, and remember that workers are paid a subsistence wage, investment is equal to the wage earners' current consumption. In fact, in the classical approach, the same goods comprise the consumption of wage earners and the investment of capitalists. As Adam Smith said: 'What is annually saved is as regularly consumed as what is annually spent and nearly in the same time too; but it is consumed by a different set of people' (Smith 1993 [1776], book I, chapter 4: 34).

While the classical school, motivated by realism as well as by reasons of image, had assumed real wages to be paid in advance, analytical considerations push the neoclassical school to prefer the opposite assumption of real wages being paid at the end of the production process.

The pivot of the neoclassical model is the marginal theory of distribution. For an equilibrium position to prevail, producers should have found out the optimal set of products (optimal quantities to be produced of each commodity), as well as an optimal resource allocation. Since, in an equilibrium position, each resource is paid according to its marginal product, this implies that labour, as well as all other resources, can only be paid when the productive process has been completed and the product has been sold on the market. Of course one could argue that wages and other rewards are determined beforehand on the basis of past experience. But this can be argued of a stationary economy; if the economy is changing, the level of the marginal products cannot be deduced from past experience (this point is analysed in greater detail in Graziani 1994).

If rigorously defined, the marginal theory of distribution can therefore only apply to an economy in which resources get their remuneration only after production has been completed. This point was seen most clearly by Alfred Marshall, when he said that 'Capital in general and labour in general co-operate in the production of the national dividend and draw from it their earnings in the measure of their respective (marginal) efficiencies.'[3]

Once the principle of wages paid in advance is abandoned in favour of a theory of wages paid at the end of the productive process, new and noteworthy analytical consequences emerge. If wages are no longer paid in advance, production can be realised without any previous saving. The contrast between a capitalist class taking care of saving and investment and a working class condemned to live at the subsistence level disappears. What in the classical approach used to be called investment, namely the subsistence advanced to wage earners, simply disappears from the model and the very term 'investment' acquires a new meaning, in that it now indicates the portion of the national product produced in the form of capital goods.

In the neoclassical model, decisions to save and to invest are no longer made by the same set of agents, as in the classical model, being respectively taken by savers and investors acting in a totally independent fashion. The problem then

---

[3] Marshall 1961 [1920], book VI, chapter 2, §10: 544. It is interesting to note that Marshall, in line with the marginal principle, rejects the concept of a fixed wage fund. However, when commenting on industrial production, he tends to consider wages as paid in advance. His argument is, though, rather weak: industrial production, he says, in contrast to agriculture, does not proceed through yearly crops but by way of a synchronised cycle. This means that at the beginning of each production cycle, the amount produced in the previous cycle is already available and can be used for paying wages to workers engaged in the following cycle (ibid., chapter 2, n. 6 and appendix J). A similar solution, while unobjectionable in itself, leaves unexplained the payment of wages at the beginning of the first cycle.

arises of ascertaining whether a mechanism exists by which the market brings saving and investment to equality. No such problem exists in the classical model, where capitalists as a class decide independently the share of net output to be saved and used as a wage fund. In the new model some form of mechanism equilibrating the respective choices of savers and investors has to be found.

Let us neglect the solution given by Walras in what fundamentally is the model of a barter economy and let us consider the problem in the framework of a monetary economy. It was Wicksell who first raised the problem and provided a full solution to it.

It should be recalled that Wicksell, while following the marginal theory of distribution, does not abandon the typical assumption of the classical model, according to which real wages are paid in advance. Just as the classical authors used to do, Wicksell imagines that, at the beginning of the production period, an amount of consumption goods is available, having been produced in the previous period and saved (in Wicksell's simplified model, savers are at the same time traders, or shop-keepers, and are indicated by the generic term 'capitalists').

Wicksell imagines as a starting point that no money is present in the economy. All means of payment are provided by the banks, which supply the money that a monetary economy needs for exchanges to take place. In Wicksell's model, bank credit is granted only to producers and not to wage earners. Money is created by the banks in order to satisfy the liquidity demands of producers. The money stock appears as a strictly endogenous variable.

Producers begin production thanks to bank credit and use it to pay wages and buy labour. Wage earners spend their money on consumer goods from traders (capitalists). The equality between demand and supply determines the level of money prices on the market for consumer goods. The money initially created by the banks is now in the hands of traders (capitalists), who pay it into their bank deposits in order to earn interest.

Let us now examine the equilibrium conditions. As we know, the equilibrium condition set by Wicksell is that monetary and real interest should be equal. In equilibrium, capital is paid according to its marginal product. In a neoclassical equilibrium (where constant returns prevail or where all firms are producing at their minimum average cost) Euler's theorem applies. This means that real wages will also be equal to the marginal product of labour. Therefore, in equilibrium, in spite of wages being paid in advance, the real wage rate satisfies the marginal rule of distribution.

Two typical features of Wicksell's model should be recalled:

a)  The loans initially granted to producers by the banks are used for paying the wage bill, a magnitude corresponding, in the terminology of the classical model, to the money value of investment. We can conclude therefore that bank loans correspond to the investments of producers.

b)  Real savings of capitalists are converted into money and into bank deposits. We can say therefore that bank deposits correspond to savings.

The preceding conclusion is especially meaningful since it allows us to restate the condition of equality between savings and investment in terms of banking operations and to say that, for savings to equal investment, banks should finance investments by loans not exceeding the amount of savings that the same banks have collected as deposits.

Wicksell analyses the conditions allowing such an equilibrium to prevail and concludes that the savings–investment equality is reached if the money interest rate set by the banks equals the natural rate of interest, a rate measuring the real return from investment. This is, however, an aspect of Wicksell's model which goes beyond the problem we are now

examining. Wicksell's model shows that a monetary economy, provided that the banking system behaves correctly, is
able to reach an equilibrium position identical in its substance to a barter equilibrium and having stable money prices.
In a similar economy, the typical feature of a monetary economy (the neutrality of money) is no longer due to *ad hoc*
assumptions, such as the exogenous nature of the money supply and equiproportional variations in all individual money
balances: it appears in fact as the spontaneous product of the
working of a market economy, with the only condition that
each agent should behave correctly (agents should observe
the budget constraint, banks should not lend more than they
have collected). The same is true of the requirements concerning monetary stability.

## 2.4   A weak point of the neoclassical formulation

The conclusions reached by Wicksell are strictly connected
to the structure of his model, and in particular to his basic
assumptions: (a) real wages are paid in advance; (b) an initial
stock of consumption goods is present, equal in amount to
the savings of the previous period as well as to investment of
the current period and to the wage bill in real terms; (c) the
initial stock of consumption goods is sold to wage earners;
the yield of the sale is paid into a bank deposit.

The neoclassical model starts from a totally different set
of assumptions which preclude the results reached in the
Wicksellian model: (a) when a production cycle is started
no previous fund of finished commodities, made possible by
past savings, is present, neither in kind nor in monetary form;
(b) productive resources get their rewards at the end of the
productive process; (c) investment is not defined as being
equal to the anticipated real wage bill but as newly produced
capital goods.

Followers of the neoclassical school abandoned the assumption of a wage paid in advance and assumed wages to

be paid at the end of the production process; but, writing themselves in Wicksell's wake, they thought it legitimate to preserve Wicksell's conclusions as to the correspondence between the categories of saving and bank deposits on the one side and investment and bank loans on the other. It is in fact an idea common to all neoclassical authors that banks collect savings by accepting deposits and that, by granting loans, they finance investment; similarly, on policy grounds, it is a common idea that banks should never grant loans exceeding the amount of deposits they have previously collected. The conclusion is that equilibrium between saving and investment is in the hands of the banks.[4]

A similar reconstruction of the macroeconomic process is invalidated by an inconsistency as well as by a real error. The inconsistency lies in the idea that savings generated in one period can be used as a resource for production to be realised in a subsequent period. That idea is correct only in the framework of the classical model, a model in which, wages being paid in advance in real terms, a previous saving in kind has to be assumed as existing at the beginning of each period. The typical neoclassical formulation, by assuming that wages are paid at the end of the production process, rules out the presence of any previous saving.

The mistake consists in the idea, to which neoclassical writers are deeply attached, that it is the duty of a serious banking system to limit the amount of loans being granted to the amount of deposits made by savers and previously collected by the banks. It is clear that, if applied to the banking system as a whole, such a prescription is untenable, since it is technically impossible for the banking system as a whole to collect deposits without having at the same time granted loans for the same amount. While in chronological terms the

---

[4] The preceding are largely accepted propositions which were defended with special emphasis by Cannan (1921) and Hayek (1935). On the other hand, it is equally well known that the same propositions also met severe criticism from Schumpeter (1954, part IV, chapter 8, §7: 110ff.).

emergence of a deposit is simultaneous with the emergence of a loan, in logical terms loans precede deposits (this point will be recalled later in this chapter and analysed in greater detail in §4.1). This mistake, concerning banking technique more than economic theory proper, invalidates the whole treatment of the savings–investment equilibrium found in the neoclassical model.

## 2.5  Inflation tax

A conclusion of the neoclassical model is that, while a perfectly competitive market is able to ensure the orderly working of a monetary economy, the working of the economy becomes unsettled when the market is manipulated by external forces.

The first source of possible manipulations is the violation of the budget constraint. In the neoclassical perspective, the budget constraint should be observed not only by single agents but also by the government sector. In principle, for a monetary equilibrium to obtain, the government's current expenditure should be financed entirely by the tax revenue, any current deficit being ruled out. On this last point two remarks are in order.

In the first place, a deficit in the government budget is consistent with the general rule of keeping a balanced government budget when, as is the rule, agents wanting protection against uncertainty and wanting to satisfy a general need for liquidity, decide to set aside a certain amount of money. If legal tender is the only kind of money, it is unavoidable that government expenditure will exceed the tax revenue by an amount exactly equal to the amount of money demanded by the public. In this case, money balances appear to be a commodity that the government supplies in order to meet a demand coming from the market and yielding a special kind of utility. We are in the presence of a sort of barter, in which the government yields legal tender, of which the government is the only producer, and gets in exchange real goods. A rigorous definition of the situation could also be that, in this case, even if an accounting deficit is present, the government is in fact running a balanced budget, since the real goods acquired by an expenditure higher than the tax revenue have been regularly paid for by selling in exchange the very special kind of commodity represented by legal tender. In this perspective, no conflict would be present between the general rule requiring a balanced budget for any agent and the presence of liquid balances kept by private agents.

A different case obtains if the government increases its deficit financed by money creation while no increase in money balances is required by the public. In this case, the rule of a balanced budget is clearly violated. The excess money created by the government deficit is no longer kept in the liquid balances of the public but spent on the market. In the framework of the neoclassical model, the consequence is an increase in prices. Wage earners experience a reduction in real income while a corresponding amount of commodities is acquired by the government. We have here a typical case of *inflation tax*. Since money prices are increased in proportion to the increase in the stock of money, the total money stock in real terms is unchanged. However, the amount of real goods that wage earners are able to buy is reduced in proportion to the increase in money prices and those agents who decide to keep their money holdings unchanged in nominal terms are hit by the increase in money prices which reduces the purchasing power of their liquid balances.

The possibility cannot be ruled out that the government uses the budget deficit financed by means of money creation in order to increase transfers to households (state pensions, subsidies, and the like). In this case, the non-government sector as a whole experiences no loss in terms of commodities. However a redistribution of real income takes place within the private sector, in favour of those agents being assigned a subsidy and against the remaining ones.[5]

## 2.6  The neoclassical theory of banking

The neoclassical theory of banking is strictly connected to the neoclassical theory of money so far sketched. In contrast to neoclassical monetary theory, nowadays largely abandoned, the principles of the neoclassical theory of banking are widely accepted, even if often in an unconscious and implicit way. A possible explanation lies in the fact that the theory of banking commonly accepted in macroeconomic theory is on most occasions a mere transposition of the microeconomic theory of the bank. It is hardly necessary to add that, as will become clear later (§2.7), the dominant theory of banking is totally different from the one adopted in the circulation approach.

In the dominant approach, the major role of a bank is of collecting savings and financing investment. In fact, a bank is generally defined as an intermediary between savers and investors. This fundamental idea lies at the basis of the main theorems of the neoclassical theory of banking:

i)    collecting deposits is a prior event with respect to granting loans: a time-honoured idea, often rejected but as often ready to be revived;

ii)   since the equality between savings and investment depends on the correct behaviour of the banks, the banking system is responsible for the entire macroeconomic equilibrium;

---

[5] The foregoing is the neoclassical reading of an inflation tax. As we shall see in more detail later (§5.4), as soon as we abandon the neoclassical model in favour of the circulation approach, the conclusions are substantially altered. In the circulation approach, producers, being able to determine the level and the nature of total output (consumer goods plus investment goods), can also determine the desired level of real profits. As a consequence, the so-called inflation tax hits only wage earners.

iii)    if the banks, violating the rule, finance investment be-
        yond the amount of available savings, a disequilibrium
        is created, the elimination of which is only possible
        by fully restoring the previous equilibrium position
        (Hayek 1933, chapter 4; 1935: 27).

It has already been noticed (§2.3) that in Wicksell's model,
and in his model only, a correspondence exists between the
pairing savings and investment on one side and the pairing
bank deposits and bank loans on the other. But, as already explained, the correspondence disappears as soon as one drops
the fundamental assumption, which Wicksell draws from the
classical model, that real wages are paid in advance, that is
before the production process is started.

In the neoclassical model, where real wages are assumed
to be paid after the completion of the production process, the
Wicksellian correspondence no longer applies. Wages being
not paid in advance, no stock of consumer goods is needed
in order to start production. Since no previous saving has
been set aside in real terms in the previous period, it is also
impossible for savings to be converted into bank deposits.
It is indeed a peculiarity of neoclassical authors that, while
dropping the assumption of real wages being paid in advance,
they keep the idea of a pre-existing fund of real savings and
bank deposits. This is all the more strange since, as will be
shown in what follows, it is technically impossible for the
banking system to collect deposits without granting at least
one loan at the same time (see chapter 5).

Let us now examine in greater detail the neoclassical doctrine of banking in its various propositions.

## Bank deposits and savings

In the traditional theory of banking, any commercial bank
takes care of collecting savings. Any increase in the amount
of bank deposits is originated by a flow of savings entrusted
to the banks.

A similar reconstruction is unobjectionable, so far as a single agent is concerned. The income of any individual is shared among consumption expenditure, durable goods, securities and bank deposits. All income not spent on consumer goods, including income used for increasing bank deposits, is in the nature of saving (more precisely, any increase in bank deposits is in the nature of monetary savings).

Just as any other form of saving, the decision to place a portion of one's savings in a bank deposit contains a speculative element since no one can foresee on what terms monetary savings will be converted into real goods at a later moment. An element of risk is present in any form of saving. Savers placing their savings in a bank deposit run the special kind of risk that inflation will reduce the real value of any monetary saving.

If, following the neoclassical approach, a full employment equilibrium is assumed, any saver deciding to increase his own bank deposit acquires a special kind of commodity having the benefit of high liquidity; but if he decides to dissave and convert his bank deposit into real goods, his decision will bring about an increase in money prices with no increase in real output. If, by way of an assumption, all savers place the same fraction of their wealth in liquid balances and all decide at the same moment to turn their money balances into real goods, the result will be an increase in money prices that, by reducing in the same proportion the real wealth of each of them, turns out to be perfectly neutral.

If an agent enjoys a monetary income enabling him to pay his saving, or a portion of it, into a bank deposit, this means that some other agent has made a monetary payment to him. This also means that the last agent, or some other one, has been granted a bank loan enabling him to make a monetary payment. This last agent can be a producer who has gone into debt with a bank for the sake of paying wages and salaries, or the government going into debt with the central bank in order to pay salaries or pensions to government employees.

Therefore any bank deposit created or increased by the monetary saving of one agent corresponds necessarily to a bank loan granted to some other agent. Any credit that a saver as a depositor claims vis-à-vis a bank corresponds to a debt incurred to a bank by some other agent.

The same problem considered under a macroeconomic viewpoint appears to be slightly different. The fact that some agents have placed their savings in a bank deposit creates as a consequence the presence of liquid balances in their favour and the corresponding presence of a bank debt for other agents. One could say therefore that it is the decision taken by a saver to keep savings in a bank deposit that produces the existence of a corresponding amount of money. Therefore, if we consider the economic system as a whole, the fact of collecting bank deposits produces no increase in the flow of savings. Its only meaning is that savings are embodied into a specific technical form which, instead of producing a higher capital formation, brings about only a higher level of liquid balances and a correspondingly higher bank debt for producers.

### Bank loans and investment

According to the dominant doctrine of banking, the role of bank loans is one of financing investment. As will be shown (§3.5), the counterpart of real investment is always real saving; therefore real investment should always be considered as being financed by real saving, never by bank credit. It is, however, worthwhile to revisit the same problem from the viewpoint of commercial banks.

It is clear that banks can never buy commodities for themselves by using their own loans: if they did so, they would violate the fundamental rule of a market economy that a promise of payment by the buyer can never constitute a final payment. Banks can instead, just as any other economic agent, and within the limits set by the legislation of each individual country, make use of realised profits to buy durable goods: commercial banks are in fact most often the owners of the buildings in which they carry on their own business and, according to the legislation of an increasing number of countries, they are entitled to place a fraction of their wealth in shares of manufacturing companies. Therefore banks can invest as any other agent, but their investments are not financed by the credit they themselves grant.

Moreover, it might happen, and most times it does happen, that pending loans are present, namely loans granted to producers and not yet repaid. More specifically, it may happen that producers, while appearing as the owners of newly produced capital goods (buildings, machinery, stocks of semi-finished products), have bank debts pending, possibly for the same amount. At the same time, a corresponding amount of liquid balances held by other agents will be present. Of course in this case, owing to the presence of a bank debt, the net wealth of producers will be lower than the value of capital goods of which they are the owners. However, so far as the savings–investment equilibrium is concerned, the situation is not changed: the value of the newly produced capital goods has a counterpart in an equivalent amount of monetary savings. If producers have bank debts pending, this does not mean that savings are lower than investment nor that a part of current investment has been financed by the banks. It only means that a portion of savings has been placed in bank deposits and that the banks are financing producers for the amount of loans that (as a consequence of the increase in demand for deposits) they have been unable to repay. Also in this case, as always, the banks are not financing investment but supplying liquidity to the economy, this being the role that the banks are supposed to perform.

### Savings–investment equilibrium

The neoclassical school, by assuming that the banking system should first collect deposits in order to be able to grant loans, ends up with the following unavoidable conclusions:

a)   A correct rule of bank behaviour, and the only one sup-
     porting a macroeconomic equilibrium, is that loans may
     not exceed the amount of deposits previously collected.
b)   If the banks observe this rule of behaviour and their
     action is no more than a transmission of liquidity from
     savers to investors, the result will be that the presence
     of the banks leaves the quantity of money unaltered. In
     the words of F.A. Hayek, the banks 'must never allow
     the effective amount of money in circulation to change'
     (Hayek 1935: 27).
c)   If the banks violate the rule, their action will bring about
     an excess of investment over saving with a consequent
     macroeconomic disequilibrium. In addition to that, the
     same banks, having granted loans in a greater amount
     than the deposits they have collected, will experience a
     shortage of liquidity and this will be in itself an incen-
     tive to reduce the scale of their operations and revert to
     a correct management.

These are the conclusions reached by the most authoritative neoclassical authors (Hayek 1935; Fanno 1992 [1933]).
Equally authoritative authors, belonging to non-neoclassical
schools (Schumpeter 1934 [1911]; Hahn 1920; Keynes 1971
[1930]), however, reach exactly opposite conclusions:

a)   It is not a duty, and even less a possibility, for the banks
     to ensure equality between savings and investment. In
     fact, since loans make deposits and not vice versa, it
     would be technically wrong to instruct the banks to
     lend no more than they have collected. Loans and de-
     posits are simultaneously determined and, if anything,
     loans have a logical priority over deposits. As for the
     savings–investment equilibrium, all that banks can be
     expected to do is to limit loans to the amount of sav-
     ings that agents' decisions, as a consequence of bank
     loans and of distributed incomes, can be expected to
     generate. It is clear, however, that the banks cannot con-
     trol how much saving is generated; this would require

knowledge and information far beyond that which a regular bank possesses.

b)    The condition for the quantity of money to be constant is not that the banks should limit their loans to the amount of previously collected savings, but that income receivers place the whole of their savings in securities, thus leaving their money balances unchanged and allowing producers entirely to repay their bank debt.

c)    Finally, the same authors emphasise the fact that a possible excess of investment over savings does not bring about any shortage of liquidity for the banks. Deposits are originated by the loans granted by the banks themselves; as a consequence, the higher the loans, the higher will be deposits. A single bank can experience all sorts of liquidity problems, but the same is not true of the banking system as a whole, since if a bank is short of liquidity there must be at least another bank having an equal amount of excess liquidity. Even individual problems of single banks are absent provided, as Keynes would say, that the the banks 'move forward in step' (Keynes 1971 [1930], chapter 1: 26) and their market share in the deposit market is unaltered.

## 2.7  Money and banking in the neoclassical model

The neoclassical theory of money, as previously outlined, may seem to be in contrast to the neoclassical theory of the bank, since if, in a rigorously defined equilibrium position, bank money is no longer present, the banks themselves should disappear. In fact, the usual presentation of the macroeconomic model, the famous IS–LM scheme, while containing the money stock as a fundamental magnitude, abstracts completely from the banking sector. In most elementary presentations of macroeconomics, the basic features of macroeconomic equilibrium are outlined without even mentioning the role of the banks. The problems of the banking sector are postponed until a later chapter where banking activity is dealt with from the viewpoint of management rather than as a problem of macroeconomic equilibrium.

More recently, a similar approach has been questioned by followers of the circuit approach, who have claimed that a stricter connection should be established between the analysis of banking and macroeconomic equilibrium. This implies that the existing stock of money should not be limited to the amount of money balances possibly existing in a theoretical Walrasian equilibrium but should be extended to cover money existing out of equilibrium, when payments are being made and agents have debts still pending towards the banks.

This implies a parallel extension of the very definition of the demand for money. Ever since the celebrated article by J.R. Hicks of 1935, the demand for money has been defined as the demand for a stock of liquidity to be kept against contingencies (the famous Keynesian bridge between the present and the future, Keynes 1973d [1937]): in the circulation approach instead, the demand for money is defined as the demand for an amount of means of payment to be used in current market exchanges – what Robertson once called the demand for money coming from 'people who want to use it' (Robertson 1937: 432).

The fact of having ignored for so long the analysis of money as a means of current payments is not without consequences. In fact, as we shall see in what follows, the definition of the demand for money as a demand for liquid balances is adopted without entirely revising the neoclassical theory of money and banking. As a consequence, in the new approach a number of inconsistent aspects emerge, the main ones being the following:

i)   As already said, and as clearly implied by the quantity equation, the required stock of money is proportional to the whole amount of goods being exchanged in the

market and to their money prices (the velocity of circulation being given). Instead, all recent models including
the banking sector are still based on the idea that the
credit requirements of producers *are only connected to
their investment decisions*. As previously remarked, a
similar idea hides a confusion between the problem of
*financing production* (namely of creating an adequate
amount of liquidity for inputs and outputs to be circulated in the market) and *financing investment* (namely
creating an equal amount of overall saving). The confusion between *initial* and *final* finance is still widespread
in the literature.

ii)   Some authors, in search of a reconciliation between the
two different meanings of initial and final finance, sug-
gest a sort of historical compromise. In their view, in the
initial stages of industrial development, the 'scarcity of
saving' would keep producers out of the financial market and force them to finance investment by means of
bank credit; in the later stages of industrial development, a rich financial market would allow investors to
obtain long-term finance by issuing securities. It will be
shown in what follows that the problem of investment
finance has little to do with the stage of development
(§3.5).

iii)   A further widespread idea is that the difference between
the neoclassical and the Keynesian models lies, among
other things, in the fact that the first one assumes savings
to be a prerequisite for investment, while in the second
the converse is true. It has been shown instead that the
justification for assuming the priority of saving lies not
in the structure of the model but in an assumption concerning the labour market, and precisely on the fact of
implicitly assuming real wages to be paid in advance.

As previously explained, if we want to introduce bank
credit and money used for current payments into the model,

we can imagine the market mechanism to be working through a number of successive phases as illustrated in §1.8. When the operations begin, no money is present. When producers have been granted the amount of bank credit they need, the liquidity reservoir of the market is full. As wage earners spend their money earnings in the commodity market, producers get back the money initially paid and can repay their bank debts. If and when all initial loans have been repaid, the liquidity reservoir is again empty. If wage earners keep a part of their earnings in their liquid balances, that amount of money stays in existence and producers are forced to carry over to the next period a bank debt of the same amount.

The typical neoclassical model considers the economy in a state of final equilibrium, when liquidity created for current payments has been used and the reservoir is empty (or semi-empty, if some liquid balances remain in existence). Models belonging to the circulation approach instead often consider the economy in the initial phase, when bank loans have just been granted to producers and the reservoir is full. In the actual working of a market economy, new production processes are continually started, which means that new loans are continually granted while old loans are continually extinguished. In a stationary economy, the amount of liquidity currently created equals the amount currently destroyed and the stock of money in existence is constant.

# 3

# A monetary economy

## 3.1 The definition of a monetary economy

It seems proper to begin by defining what is meant respectively by a barter economy, a credit economy, and a monetary economy.

### A barter economy

By a barter economy we mean an economy in which commodities are directly exchanged against other commodities. It should be immediately remarked that an exchange of commodities without any intermediation of money does not necessarily imply that the delivery of the two commodities being exchanged is simultaneous. In ancient times, it might be customary to borrow seed and to repay by delivering a given amount of wheat after the crop. This would be a case of an exchange assisted by credit in the framework of a barter economy.

A step forward is the case of an economy using one single commodity, for instance gold, as a general intermediary of exchange and as a unit of measurement of prices. In this case, the economy is using a commodity money. However, it still falls in the category of a barter economy, since the commodity money is privately produced along with all other commodities. Of course a similar economy would be technically more advanced compared with the more primitive cases of economies in which single commodities are directly exchanged one against the other.

A barter economy can be an economy of direct producers, where no wage labour is present (the case of slave labour is of course totally different). If production is carried on by individuals or families owning their own pieces of land, any such producer, by selling the product of that land, is able to acquire commodity money that will be used in order to buy commodities produced by others. A barter economy can also be making use of wage labour. If wages are paid in advance, producers need commodity money in order to pay the wage bill. The money can be supplied by agents having saved in the form of commodity money a part of their income. The case of a barter economy in which wages are paid in advance comes as close as possible to the neoclassical idea of an economy in which savings necessarily precede investment (§2.3).

Since the presence of a commodity money does not turn a barter economy into a monetary economy, we can conclude that a true monetary economy necessarily makes use of a token money.

## A credit economy

In a credit economy commodities are exchanged against simple promises of payment accepted by each agent on the basis of mutual confidence. In this case, each act of exchange gives rise to a bilateral credit–debt relationship between single agents. A simplified example might be the case of an economy in which all payments are performed by means of bills of exchange having the same maturity date. If all agents act within their own budget constraints, when the moment comes in which payments are due, bills in existence will be perfectly compensated and all debts simultaneously settled.

More than one author is inclined to consider a credit economy as substantially similar to a monetary economy in which credit performs the role of money (Hawtrey 1931; Heinsohn and Steiger 1983; Screpanti 1993: 85ff.). Others, and among those the followers of the circuit approach, prefer to preserve a clear distinction between a credit economy and a monetary economy. In fact in a credit economy commodities circulate against promises of payment, creating a debt relationship between the two agents, which means that credit, while being a means of exchange, is not a means of payment and does not give rise to a final cancellation of the debt (this point is especially emphasised by Riese 1998: 47). If, when the payment comes due, bills are not totally extinguished, the debtors are held to satisfy the pending debts, which means that so far only promises of payment have been made but no actual payment has taken place. If a simple promise of payment could perform the role of a final payment, buyers would be endowed with a seigniorage privilege, namely with a right of withdrawing goods from the market without giving anything in exchange (a similar case is imagined by Mark Twain in his tale 'The Million Pound Note').

### A monetary economy

The preceding remarks lead to the conclusion that a monetary economy should not make use of a commodity money nor of simple promises of payment. A real money should satisfy three main characteristics:

i)   since money cannot be a commodity, it can only be a token money;

ii)  the use of money must give rise to an immediate and final payment and not to a simple commitment to make a payment in the future; and

iii) the use of money must be so regulated as to give no privilege of seigniorage to any agent.

The only system of payments satisfying the above three conditions is one in which payments go through a third party acting as an intermediary (a description not far from the present one is given by Cartelier 2001: 165). In modern times, the intermediary is usually a bank. When an agent makes a payment by means of a bank cheque, if his bank approves the operation, his counterpart is credited with the amount due and no debt remains pending *between the two agents*. Debts and credits do remain pending between each one of the agents involved and their own banks: precisely, the buyer becomes a debtor of his own bank and the seller a creditor. The fact that no direct debt remains pending between the two agents is a guarantee of the fact that the means of payment being used is in the true nature of money. At the same time, the fact that debt and credit relationships remain pending between each of the agents and his own bank is a guarantee of the fact that none of them is granted seigniorage privileges (De Vecchi 1993, part II, chapter 5, §1).

We can conclude that, in order for all the requirements of a monetary economy to be satisfied, any payment should take place *in the form of a triangular transaction*. In De Vecchi's words: 'who has contributed to production . . . is credited with a claim [issued by a central social accounting body] which can be used to purchase whatever commodity he likes' (De Vecchi 1993: 64; also Schmitt 1975: 14; Cencini 1984: 31; Parguez 1985; Padoa Schioppa 1989; Berti 1992).[1]

Money, not being a commodity, is in the nature of credit. However, it is not a direct credit between the two contracting agents, but an indirect relationship set up by means of a triangular transaction in which a third agent acts as an intermediary. Coined metal money, while having the appearance of a commodity money, is also in the nature of credit money. As Keynes once wrote, the Indian rupee is 'a note printed on

[1] Riese would add one further requirement, namely that, in order for a true monetary economy to exist, similar triangular transactions should be the regular practice of the market. In this case, being an intermediary of exchange becomes a regular professional activity and intermediaries (typically the banks) compete in order to attract customers. It so happens that banks, instead of asking for a payment, may offer a reward to agents making use of their services and opening deposits with them (Riese 1992).

silver' (Keynes 1971 [1913], chapter 3: 26; the same conclusion is reached by Schumpeter, 1934 [1911]: 45ff.).

The role of money is not only one of replacing a number of single bilateral barters by a general multilateral exchange, but also of making barter no longer necessary and eliminating it altogether. In a monetary economy, any agent can sell without immediately buying. Money makes it possible for buyers to defer sales and vice versa; in the interval between sale and purchase the agent has at his disposal a stock of liquid resources. Money is therefore at the same time and for the same reasons a means of payment, a liquid balance (and therefore a form of wealth), and a form of debt.

## 3.2  Money as a triangular relationship

The definition of a monetary payment as the result of a triangular relationship, far from being a mere theoretical construction, satisfies the basic requirement that the use of a token money should not allow agents to enjoy seigniorage privileges.

This explains why the rules applying to single individuals also apply to commercial banks so far as their mutual payments are concerned. Indeed, if commercial banks made their reciprocal payments by means of bank deposits they would be acting as in a credit economy; conversely, if a payment made by means of a bank deposit were considered as final, this would again open the possibility of seigniorage privileges. In order for commercial banks to act in a regime of monetary payments without undue privileges, payments among commercial banks have to be intermediated by a third agent, being usually a central bank (Hawtrey 1931: 545–7). In principle, the same procedure might apply to payments among central banks, if a world bank were established. Since no such institution exists, central banks can only settle their relationships in one of two ways: (a) by means of mutual credits, while waiting for compensation of their mutual debt and credit relationships; or (b) by means of barter, namely by using a commodity money that nowadays still consists in gold bars.[2]

A central bank is needed in order to perform at least two main roles:

i)  it should ensure that each commercial bank observes its own budget constraint;

ii) at the same time a central bank should monitor the commercial banks and prevent them from spontaneously expanding credit 'in step' (by so doing, the banks could avoid individual problems of liquidity while allowing aggregate demand to increase with the consequent dangers of inflationary pressure).

In contrast to the preceding view, a school of thought exists according to which a system of monetary exchange could work without trouble by means of private monies, produced by single banks offering their payment services. Single agents would freely choose among the various banks after evaluating their status and solidity. According to this approach, a modern market could work without problems in the absence of a commodity money and also in the absence of any legal tender. Similar views perpetuate the idea, held by Carl Menger, that money is the spontaneous product of the market. In this perspective, the presence in each national market of one single legal tender officially recognised as a means of settling debts can only be due to an imposition of the government carried on by means of legal restrictions aimed at protecting the legal tender issued by the central bank (White 1984; McCallum 1985).

---

[2] In the international market a commodity money is still present today. It is worth noting that economists belonging to the Marxist tradition emphasise this aspect as confirming the general principle that in a capitalistic economy, where value is determined by the labour content of each commodity, only a commodity money can be used as a measuring rod of value (De Brunhoff 1976 [1967]).

Similar ideas are based on the implicit assumption that the banking sector is fully competitive and capable of self-regulation. However, as Keynes had already noticed (Keynes 1971 [1930], vol. I, chapter 2, §1), even in the absence of any explicit collusion, a system of private banks might give rise to an unlimited expansion of credit. It seems therefore that a system based on paper money has to be monitored by a central bank, the only one enabled to issue a currency officially considered as legal tender. A similar monitoring system can only originate from a decision taken at the political level.

## 3.3  The creation of money

Let us imagine a perfectly competitive credit market, in which agents are able to get credit provided they are prepared to pay the prevailing rate of interest, in the absence of uncertainty. In similar conditions, no agent would go into debt with a bank unless the moment had come to make a payment, since there is no reason to pay interest just for the sake of keeping idle an unnecessary liquid balance. This is a widely recognised point (Keynes 1973a [1936]: 96; 1973b [1937]: 208; 1973c [1937]: 223; Barrère 1979: 127 and 1988b: 41). If an agent decides to keep an idle balance, and meets the cost consequent to his decision, this means that he has to face some sort of uncertainty: he may feel uncertain about the possibility of getting in the future the same amount of credit, or about the rate of interest that will be demanded.[3]

In this respect, the followers of the circulation approach add a second remark. Let us imagine that agents, wanting protection against uncertainty, decide to build up a liquid balance to cover payments to be made in the near future, and that, in order to avoid risks of default, they are willing to pay

---

[3] Riese suggests a similar idea by saying that a demand for liquid balances appears when the monetary authorities or the banking sector make credit artificially scarce (Riese 1998).

interest on the idle balances in their possession. The result is that, in the interval between the moment the bank grants them credit and the moment they actually make use of it, the same agents have at the same time a debt towards the bank and, being the owners of a deposit, a credit towards the same bank. Since the two positions cancel each other out, no net creation of money has taken place. The conclusion is that no money creation is possible unless a payment is made: money is created only at the moment in which a payment is actually performed. When a payment is made, money is created and two debt relationships emerge: the agent making a payment becomes a debtor while whoever receives the payment becomes a creditor of the banking system.[4]

Since in a monetary economy any payment between two agents necessarily involves a third agent recognised as a producer of means of payment, any model of a monetary economy must consider banks and firms as two separate sets of agents. Firms produce commodities and make use of banks in order to make the payments they need to; the banks provide means of payment and act as clearing houses between the contracting agents. In any case, banks and firms cannot be aggregated into the same sector.

What has been said of the triangular transactions giving rise to monetary payments applies to all sorts of channels by which money can be created, namely refinancing granted by the central bank to commercial banks, government

---

[4] Different readings have been given of the process of money creation by authors subscribing to the circulation approach. Most authors would say that money is created by the banking system turning a private promise of payment into a means of payment generally accepted in the market. In this line, Parguez defines money as a private promise of payment endorsed by a bank (Parguez 1984: 98). Bernard Schmitt conversely considers the banking system as capable only of granting credit and not of creating money. In his view, money can emerge only from an agreement reached between the two contracting agents, according to which the bank is considered as sponsor of the payment. Therefore money is created not by the bank but by the agents themselves, the moment they decide to consider the bank as the ruler of their mutual payments (Schmitt 1984, chapter 4: 110).

expenditure not covered by taxes or by issues of new government bonds, or, in an open economy, a balance of payments surplus. When the monetary base is supplied by the central bank to a commercial bank, money is created when one bank goes into debt to the central bank in order to repay a debt to another bank. In this case, the three agents are the two commercial banks and the central bank. When the monetary base is supplied by a commercial bank to a single agent, money is created when one agent goes into debt to his own bank in order to repay a debt to a second agent. In this case, the three agents are the bank and the two contracting agents. Finally, when the monetary base is supplied by the central bank to the government, money is created when the government makes a payment to a private agent. In this case, the three agents are the central bank, the government and the private agent.

## 3.4  The money supply in mainstream economics

Mainstream economics considers as typical the case in which money is created by government expenditure not covered by taxes or by issues of new government bonds (for a typical treatment see Mankiw 1992: 463–70). In fact, the typical definition of the creation of new money to be found in any handbook of macroeconomics is: $dM = G - T\, dB_G$ (where $G$ is government expenditure, $T$ is the tax yield, $dB_G$ is newly issued government bonds).

As already recalled, a similar definition, while not exhaustive of all possible sources of money creation, has a logic of its own. Let us consider a market in an equilibrium position. Let us stipulate that the equilibrium conditions include the condition that no debts are pending among single agents, and therefore not even between firms and banks. If no agent is in debt towards any bank, there are no bank loans outstanding and therefore no bank deposits created as a consequence of the banks having granted bank loans. Any amount of monetary base still in the possession of the banks has only one possible origin, namely a deficit government expenditure (or, in an open economy, a balance of payments surplus). The common definition of money creation corresponds therefore to a rigorously defined equilibrium condition.

As already remarked, the followers of the circulation approach diverge on this point (above, §1.2). They think that the working of a monetary economy should be analysed first of all in the framework of a market economy consisting only of the private sector. The creation of money is thus analysed in the absence of any government expenditure. As a consequence, the starting point of their analysis is the case in which the monetary base is created only through the refinancing operated by the central bank to meet the needs of commercial banks. Their basic model is very close to the so-called model of a *pure credit economy*, first analysed by Wicksell (1936 [1898], chapter 9, section B), Robertson (1926 and 1928) and Hawtrey (1923, chapter 1).

## 3.5   Financing production and financing investment

According to the traditional formulation of the neoclassical school, the equilibrium configuration of the economy is determined by the preferences of single agents within the constraints determined by available resources. Of course any scholar of neoclassical faith would admit that the banking system, by controlling the flow of credit, might determine a structure of production in conflict with the preferences of agents. But, by so doing, the banking system would neglect the rules of its correct working and would create a temporary situation, totally out of equilibrium and bound to be reversed sooner or later (a famous discussion between F.A. Hayek and J.M. Keynes took place on this point; Graziani 1998).

On the other hand, followers of the Keynesian approach tend to limit their analysis to the Keynesian model of the *General Theory*. At the same time, they tend to neglect almost completely his previous and later works, where Keynes deals much more extensively with problems connected to finance and to the relationships between banks and firms (Graziani 1991). The same tendency is even stronger in the post-Keynesian school, a school that, especially in the extreme formulations given by Kaldor and Moore, assumes the credit supply of banks to be infinitely elastic, thus neglecting any constraint firms might be confronted with when financing their production plans.

In the *General Theory*, Keynes, with the exception of a few isolated comments, abstracts from the main problems connected to bank credit. Keynes implicitly assumes banks and firms share the same expectations about the level of aggregate demand. As a consequence, if a firm has decided upon a given volume of production, there will also be a bank prepared to grant the required finance. A similar idea is implicit in Keynes's general assumption that, in the short run, there will be a precise correspondence between expectations and actual results (Keynes 1973a [1936], chapter 5, §2). In the short run, the firms of the *General Theory* have no problems and make no mistakes in following the pace of aggregate demand. Problems may emerge in that the rate of interest may be too high to make investment profitable, but this is due to the liquidity preference of savers, especially of *rentiers*, rather than to decisions coming from the managers of the banks.

It so happens, therefore, that, in spite of their conflicting approaches, the neoclassical and the Keynesian schools converge in overshadowing the relevance of finance and of bank behaviour. A consequence not to be neglected takes place at the analytical level, in that the problems of finance are considered only as far as investment is concerned.

Followers of the circulation approach take a totally different position. When analysing problems of finance, they make a clear distinction between *financing production* and *financing investment*. As already remarked (§2.7), the initial finance requirement of firms equals the wage bill. This already makes clear that the finance requirement of the firms must cover the cost of total production and is not confined to financing specifically the production of capital goods. As we shall see, a problem of financing investment exists, but it has little to do with the problem of getting finance from the banks. Still, since it is quite common to read in the literature that investment expenditure is, or can be, financed by bank credit and that the demand for bank credit depends on the investment plans of firms (or on their plans for increasing the level of investment), the distinction between the two kinds of finance deserves to be made clear.

## Financing production

Firms need finance in order to set up and carry on any kind of production. This kind of finance can be properly named *initial finance* and must cover the total cost of the planned amount of production, no matter what the nature of the product (consumer goods or capital goods). In fact, as John Stuart Mill once said, the distinction between capital and consumption 'does not lie in the kind of commodities but in the mind of the capitalist' (Mill 1909 [1848], book I, chapter 4: 56). Initial finance is therefore an essential element, the lack of which makes any production plan impossible (Keynes 1973c [1937]: 222; Parguez 1975: 108).

As already said, initial finance, once used for paying wages, goes back to the firms by way of the commodity market or through the financial market and is destroyed as soon as the firms repay their initial bank debt. Since the role of initial finance is to make it possible to carry out the production process, it is essentially in the nature of *temporary finance*. It is also clear on the other hand that liquid balances held by single agents are not connected to finance for production or for investment.

The liquidity collected by firms either selling commodities or issuing securities can be denominated *final finance*. In contrast to initial finance, the role of final finance is no longer to enable the production process but rather to make it possible to firms to repay their bank debt (this point had already been clearly made by Bresciani-Turroni 1936). So far as the repayment of bank debt is concerned, it makes no difference whether final finance is collected from the commodity market or from the financial market: what counts is that the sum of what is collected covers the amount of initial finance. If this condition is satisfied, firms settle their debts to the banks and can consider themselves to have reached an equilibrium position.

One aside is appropriate. If firms totally repay their bank debt at the end of each production cycle, money in existence is totally destroyed. It might be more realistic instead to imagine as a normal situation the case in which agents decide to hold, for precautionary reasons, a liquid balance that in stationary conditions can be considered as constant. If the level of activity is constant, once the equilibrium level of liquid balances is achieved, the money created at the beginning of each production cycle is regularly destroyed at the end of the same cycle, and the firms reach an equilibrium position with a constant bank debt. The same conclusion could be expressed by saying that a stationary economy is in equilibrium if the money stock is constant.

A similar conclusion is instrumental for analysing the old question concerning the determination of the money stock in the *General Theory*. Those interpreters of Keynes who tend to reconcile the Keynesian model with the more traditional way of thinking consider it an indisputable point that, in the *General Theory*, the money stock appears as a given magnitude. Those instead who tend to read Keynes as a heterodox economist attempt to demonstrate that, also in the *General Theory*, the money stock is considered by Keynes an endogenous variable. As already remarked, it cannot be ruled out that the correct interpretation lies midway; and precisely that if, in the *General Theory*, the money stock is considered a given magnitude, this does not depend, as it does in the neoclassical model, on a restrictive definition of the supply of money, but on the fact that the balance between current expenditures and current revenues of firms (and consequently, in a stationary economy, a constant bank debt) is considered to be a condition of equilibrium. If Keynes in the *General Theory* considers the money stock as constant, this should not be judged either as a way of simplifying the model or as a way of considering money as an exogenous variable. It is rather a simple definition of the equilibrium condition of the firms in a monetary economy in stationary conditions.

## Financing investment

Investment is financed the moment in which newly produced capital goods find a buyer on the market. The sale of new capital goods may take place in either of two ways:

i)   Capital goods may be sold to savers in an indirect way, namely through the sale of securities on the financial market. The typical form of this operation is the purchase by savers of equities issued by the firm. By such a purchase, savers become stockholders and therefore co-owners of the firm.

ii)  Capital goods may be exchanged among firms. This happens whenever firms having realised a profit use it to buy capital goods from the firms who produced them (it may well happen that a firm having produced a capital good decides to hold it and to make a direct use of it, thus realising its profit in kind).

Since either of the two different forms of placing new capital goods on the market implies an act of saving (be it saving coming from wage earners or from a firm), the result is that *investment finds its final finance in saving*. Saving provided by free decisions of wage earners can be named *voluntary saving*. If new capital goods are bought by firms using profits, some would prefer to define saving as *forced saving* (this point will be taken up again later, §9.3). Anyhow, we can conclude that, be it voluntary or forced saving, any investment finds its final finance in saving.[5]

This conclusion deserves a few more comments. A first possibility, already mentioned, is the case of a stationary economy with a constant demand for liquid balances. In this case, the savings of wage earners are entirely spent in the financial market and newly produced capital goods are entirely sold, either by means of securities placed in the financial market, or by means of profits earned by firms. Since wage earners spend the whole of their incomes (be it in the commodities market or in the financial market), firms are able to repay the whole of the credit granted to them by the banks. If at the very beginning of the period under consideration the firms were in debt to the banks, their debt remains constant and equal to the amount of the liquid sums held by consumers.

An apparently different case is the one in which an increase in the demand for liquid balances takes place. In this case, the savings of wage earners are partly used in order to increase bank deposits, only what remains being placed on the financial market. In this case, as already remarked, the bank debt of the firms increases by exactly the same amount by which the liquid balances of consumers have been increased. The issue of securities in the financial market attracts to the

---

[5] As Victoria Chick says, the role of saving is of funding investment, Chick 1995: 30–1. A similar reasoning, although in a different perspective, is made by Keynes (1973a [1936]: 81ff.). It is worth recalling that it is commonly, and wrongly, affirmed that the term 'forced saving' was first introduced by Ludwig von Mises (Hansson 1992: 140–1). This is, however, a highly debatable attribution, since von Mises himself, who since the first edition of his work in 1912 dealt extensively with the problems of forced saving, admitted later on that the first to use the term in the German-language literature had been Knut Wicksell (von Mises 1928, part II, §2, n.1). This point was made clear by Schumpeter (1954, part III, chapter 7, 4(a): 724, and part IV, chapter 8, §7: 1115). Even before Wicksell, the same term can be found in other Italian authors, such as De Viti De Marco (1885: 205). The complete story of the concept and of the term is told in Hayek 1932 and 1935: 18ff.

firms a sum lower than the cost of newly produced capital goods. As a consequence, the owners of the firms, namely stockholders, will notice that while the gross wealth of their firms has increased because of new plant and machinery acquired, the burden of bank debt has increased by an amount equal to the increase in liquid balances that consumers have decided to hold. In this case, investment is once more financed by savings, the only difference being that savers, in an indirect way, through the firms of which they own the stock, have gone into debt to the banks in order to increase their own liquid balances.

The conclusion just reached, namely that final finance for investment is always supplied by savings, has a special meaning in relation to the case of developing countries. According to a widespread opinion, while in advanced countries the flow of savings is always abundant, in developing countries there is never enough saving to finance private or government investment (Chick 1986; Studart 1995: 36–9, 51–4). The conclusion is often drawn that, owing to the lack of saving, investment has to be financed partly or wholly by bank credit. The preceding analysis shows that that idea is highly debatable. It is of course true that in a developing country the propensity to save is ordinarily low. But, once a given amount of investment has been planned and executed, the formation of an equal amount of saving will inevitably follow. If the propensity to save is high, savers will acquire an increase in financial wealth equal to investment; if the propensity to save is low, investment will be financed by means of forced savings and the firms will get a corresponding amount of profits. In both cases, investment will be financed by means of savings. Bank credit can only solve a different problem, namely that of making it possible for agents to hold the desired amount of liquid balances.

The case of an open economy is of course different. Here, investments higher than savings can be matched by capital imports from abroad. However, also in this case, investment is financed by savings, even if by foreign saving rather than domestic. In any case the so-called bank financing of investment can be ruled out.

## 3.6 Comments on the dominant literature

It was remarked in the preceding section that it is quite common to read in the literature that investment expenditure is, or can be, financed by bank credit and that the demand for bank credit depends on the investment plans of firms (or on their plans for increasing the level of investment). This is in fact a common aspect of most macroeconomic models which give a separate treatment of the problems concerning the credit sector.

A good example of the dominant literature is offered by the Modigliani–Papademos macroeconomic model.[6] Their model is a convenient point of reference not only because it gives ample space to the banking sector but also because the authors assume bank credit to be the only source of finance for firms. The Modigliani–Papademos model is the exact opposite of the typical macro models, where banks are neglected and the only source of finance is assumed to be the financial market.

The substance of the model can be represented by the following equations:

$$Y = W + P \tag{3.1}$$

$$W = \beta Y \tag{3.2}$$

$$P = (1 - \beta)Y \tag{3.3}$$

$$S = s(W + P) \tag{3.4}$$

$$I = (r_L) \tag{3.5}$$

$$Y = \frac{1}{s}I \tag{3.6}$$

---

[6] Modigliani and Papademos 1990: 463ff. In what follows, only those parts of the model that are relevant to the point under discussion will be considered.

$$I(r_L) - S_P = \mathrm{d}L \tag{3.7}$$

$$S_w = \mathrm{d}D_s + \mathrm{d}D = I - S_P(Y) = \mathrm{d}L \tag{3.8}$$

$$r_s = \mathrm{f}(r^*) \tag{3.9}$$

$$D/D_s = \mathrm{f}(r_s). \tag{3.10}$$

Equation (3.1) defines income as a sum of wages and profits. Equations (3.2) and (3.3) define the shares of wages and profits in national income as given. Equation (3.4) defines total savings, assuming the saving propensities of households and firms to be equal. Equation (3.5) defines investment as a function of the interest rate charged on bank loans. Equation (3.6) defines income according to the usual multiplier mechanism (the same equation implies the savings–investment equality). Equation (3.7) indicates that investment is financed partly by internal saving (reinvested profits), partly by bank credit. Equation (3.8) defines household savings as the sum of savings deposits and demand deposits (since the financial market is assumed to be absent, this is the only choice open to households). The total increase in bank deposits is defined as equal to the total increase in credit granted to firms. The equilibrium condition between the demand for credit (equal to investment) and the creation of credit by banks (equal to new deposits) determines the rate of interest on loans. Equation (3.9) indicates that the banks set the interest reckoned on savings deposits as a function of the official discount rate $r^*$ set by the central bank. Equation (3.10) defines the ratio between the demand for demand deposits and savings deposits as a function of the rate reckoned on savings deposits.

The model contains ten equations, ten unknowns and three exogenous variables (the discount rate, the propensity to save and the distribution parameter ß).

The model clearly examines the economy in its final equilibrium position. The amount of liquidity appearing in the model is therefore equal to the final amount of liquid balances (in this case bank deposits) demanded by households.

It does not consider the amount of liquidity initially created for making exchanges possible and subsequently partially destroyed. The existing amount of bank deposits also measures the bank debt of the firms.

However, such a model leaves a number of questions unanswered.

To begin with, since the model only considers a position of final equilibrium, the banks don't appear in their usual role of providing liquidity for financing current exchanges. Since the financial market is absent and bank deposits are the only possible destination of household savings, banks are instead assigned the role of financing investment.

A second anomaly is that, owing to the absence of a financial market, the whole of current savings of households is used to increase bank deposits. The usual factors determining the demand for liquid balances (current transactions, precaution, speculation) disappear.

Finally, while the counterpart of real accumulation is an increasing stock of financial wealth in the hands of savers, in this model, so far as current savings are positive, the existing bank deposits become unlimited.

In contrast to the Modigliani–Papademos model, the model formulated by Bernanke and Blinder considers both the banking sector and the financial market.[7] The authors start with a definition of the balance sheet of the banks, where deposits $D$ appear as the only liability, while loans $L$, securities $B$ and reserves $Z$ appear as assets. Therefore loans are defined as:

$$L = D - B - Z.$$

Since a reserve ratio $q$ is imposed on the banks ($Z = qD$), we can write:

$$L = (1/q - 1)Z - B.$$

[7] Bernanke and Blinder 1988.

The banks move between loans and securities according to the respective prevailing interest rates, $r_L$ and $r_B$:

$$B = B(r_L, r_B); \quad L = L(r_L, r_B).$$

Investments are also a function of the same interest rates:

$$I = I(r_L, r_B),$$

and can be financed either by issuing securities, by self-financing, or by bank credit. Therefore, the demand for bank loans on the part of the firms, $L^d$, equals investment minus new securities issued, minus self-financing. If we neglect self-financing, we can write:

$$L^d = I(r_L, r_B) - B.$$

In the credit market, the interest rate on bank loans is determined by the equality between demand and supply.

The supply of bank deposits is determined by the reserve requirements of the banks:

$$D^s = \frac{1}{q} Z,$$

while the demand for bank deposits is a function of the interest rate on securities. The equilibrium condition determines the rate of interest on securities:

$$D^d(r_B) = \frac{1}{q} Z.$$

This is very similar to the Keynesian theory of the rate of interest. Interest in the financial market is determined by liquidity preference coupled to the existing quantity of money.

This model also leaves some questions unanswered. In the model, legal tender is only used for bank reserves and bank deposits are at the same time a liquid balance for households and a bank debt of the firms. The authors consider investments to be the motive behind the demand for bank loans and therefore to be financed by bank credit. But it would be equally correct, and even more accurate, to say that investment finds its counterpart in savings and that banks are financing the demand for liquid holdings coming from households.

## 3.7   The historical origins of money

The previous definitions of money and monetary payments implicitly belie what is still today the most widespread reconstruction of the origins of money. As already noted, it is usually believed that money was originally a commodity money, consisting in a specific commodity (such as salt or cattle), chosen because of its special technical attributes, replaced later on by precious metals (such as gold or silver), again replaced by coined money (so as to eliminate uncertainty about title and weight), then by paper money as a representative of metal money, and finally by bank deposits, credit cards and electronic money. A similar theory describing the historical genesis of money as a series of gradual improvements has a long history and was endorsed by the most famous theoreticians of the last two centuries.[8]

The opponents of the traditional individualistic school, according to which the market is able spontaneously to select one commodity and make of it a commonly accepted means of payment, insist on the idea that only the law can determine what is a means of payment able to cancel a debt. As Keynes wrote '. . . it is the State . . . which decides what it is

---

[8] Galiani 1780, book 1, chapter 1; Ferrara 1961 [1856: 1ff.]; Menger 1892; Marshall 1961 [1920], appendix A; Hicks 1989: 63ff.; Clower 1977: 211. Summaries of the long debate can be found in Benetti 1991 and in Realfonzo 1998. Keynes never agreed on the traditional reconstruction (Keynes 1983 [1914]: 421, *Collected Writings*, vol. 11: 406). A similar disagreement was expressed by Schumpeter. In his view, the essential role of money is the ability to perform a payment, while the material substance is no more than an external complication imposed by the requirements of a primitive society (Schumpeter 1970: 213ff.; De Vecchi 1993: 64ff.).

that must be delivered as a lawful or customary discharge of a contract which has been concluded in terms of the money-of-account . . . This right is claimed by all modern States and has been so claimed for some four thousand years at least' (Keynes 1971 [1930]: 4).[9]

In all modern nations, the payments system is based on notes issued by the central bank or, as happens in the European Monetary Union, by a supranational central bank. This has led a number of authors to modify the very definition of money. In their view, we should not consider as money any means of payment generally accepted in the market, but only that particular means of payment which, according to the law, is considered as a means of discharging a debt. This is the famous 'state theory of money', first propounded by the German economist Friedrich Knapp (Knapp 1924 [1905]). Knapp's theory, according to which only the power of the state and not the spontaneous working of the market can turn a commodity into money, was endorsed by most authoritative authors.[10]

It might be added that the law can prescribe that a specific means of payment is able to discharge a debt, but this is not enough to make of it a means of payment in all circumstances. In fact, in spite of the law, the seller can always refuse to sell a commodity unless payment is made in a so-called strong currency (this is quite common in countries where the official means of payment recognised by the law is a weak local currency while sellers ask to be paid in strong foreign currency). What the law can do is to make a specific currency

---

[9] The same view is held today by Hajo Riese. In his view, only the law can determine how a debt is finally settled. Therefore money can only be created by an institution (in modern times, a central bank), entitled to issue legal tender (Riese 1998: 47, 56). Both Keynes and Riese build on Knapp's *State Theory of Money* (Knapp 1924 [1905]).

[10] Hawtrey 1927: 2, 1931: 545; Keynes 1971 [1930], chapter 1: 4, 6 (Keynes was also a promoter of the English translation of Knapp's book). Nowadays, the state theory of money is strongly endorsed by Hajo Riese (1998). A general review of the more recent formulations is contained in Cesarano 1995.

attractive, for instance by prescribing that the same currency must be used in order to pay taxes.[11]

The Marxian school refuses both the theory of the continuous evolution of money as determined by spontaneous choices of the market, and the theory of an unchallengeable law that can impose as money any means of payment. Orthodox Marxist scholars think that the only true kind of money is a commodity money having a labour content and therefore being a basis for measuring the value of any other commodity. A different interpretation comes from other scholars of Marxist extraction but inclined to accept the structural evolution of modern societies. In this line of thought, Heinsohn and Steiger have elaborated a special hypothesis concerning the origin of money, which brings them to accept the idea that in modern times money is in the nature of credit. Their starting point is that we no longer live in a primitive society in which the land is common property of the community, but in a capitalistic society in which means of production are private property. In ancient societies, where land is common property and the product is distributed among participants according to egalitarian criteria, no one feels the need to hold a liquid balance. If the community needs to protect itself against certain contingencies, the only possible measures are real and not monetary (protection against bad crops can only be obtained by holding a stock of wheat, while the position of the single agent whose crop has been lost will be safeguarded when the available product is distributed). The situation is completely altered with the insurgence of private property. The community is now no longer able to distribute the available product in equal shares among its

---

[11] The banker John Law, in a certain phase of his financial adventure, obtained that taxes due to the city of Paris could only be paid in notes issued by his own bank (Jannaccone 1946: 88). Similarly, Sismondi relates how the Empress Maria Theresa of Austria, in an attempt to assist the Bank of Vienna, prescribed that taxes could be paid only in notes issued by that bank (Sismondi 1919 [1819]: 11).

members and the single agent whose income accidentally declines can only go into debt in order to survive. In a similar situation, debts emerge and money makes its appearance as the general equivalent used for measuring the value of obligations over time. Since debts carry with them the obligation to pay interest, a consequence is that producers having gone into debt need to earn a profit.[12]

---

[12] Heinsohn and Steiger show how the first form of liquid balance originated from deposits in kind entrusted to convents and sanctuaries. Depositors were given receipts which circulated as money. Ancient money was therefore also credit money. The authors have revisited and refined their theory a number of times since they first formulated it (Heinsohn and Steiger 1983, 1996, 2000, 2001).

# 4

---

# The creation of bank money

## 4.1 Loans make deposits

As already noted, the circulation approach rejects the idea that deposits make loans, an idea that Schumpeter already considered an old prejudice.[1] In the circulation approach the opposite conception is adopted, namely that loans make deposits.[2]

The 'old prejudice' is based on the assumption that, without a previous collection of deposits, the banking system would be unable to make any loan since, when making loans, a bank makes use of previously collected deposits. Simple considerations of banking technique show the inconsistency of this idea. An agent opening a bank deposit doesn't lose his own liquidity, since he is usually able to make use of his

[1] Schumpeter 1954: 1110–17. Schumpeter's critique was brilliantly elaborated by his Bonn pupil Erich Schneider (1962, chapter 2, §3, n. 15).

[2] Among the authors endorsing this view the following can be noted: Hahn 1920; Robertson 1926; Keynes 1971 [1930], vol. I, chapter 2; De Viti De Marco 1990 [1934], chapter 3, §8; Marget 1966 [1938]: 160–71. J.R. Hicks, in his *Market Theory of Money*, devotes much space to the description of banking. Still it would be hard to say on which side he stands and whether he assigns a priority to loans or to deposits (Hicks 1989, chapters 6 and 7). The whole debate is critically discussed in Realfonzo 1998. The debate on the priority of loans over deposits is sometimes confused with the debate on the endogenous vs. exogenous determination of the money stock (Palley 1997: 133). As will be shown in what follows, the priority of loans over deposits is a hardly debatable principle, while it can be debated whether the monetary authorities do or do not have control of the amount of loans granted by banks and of the amount of money in existence.

deposit as a means of payment at any moment and without notice. At the same time a bank, when making a new loan, is granting additional liquidity to an agent without subtracting any liquidity from any of its own depositors. Therefore, as Hawtrey concluded, when a bank makes a loan to a customer, it is not transmitting liquidity from one agent to another one but creating new liquidity (Hawtrey 1931: 548; Schumpeter 1934 [1911], chapter 3, part I).

In a pure credit economy, in which the government sector is assumed to be absent, the principle that loans make deposits does not require any special explanation. It is in fact self-evident that if loans granted by commercial banks were totally absent, no agent would be able to make any deposit for absolute lack of liquidity. On the other hand, it is equally self-evident that, in order to grant a loan, commercial banks need not have previously collected liquidity.

It might seem that if the government sector is present, the situation might be different. But such an impression would be wrong. No doubt, an agent receiving a payment from the government can make use of the new liquidity to open a bank deposit. It might then seem that no bank loan has been previously granted and that new loans will be made possible thanks to the new deposit. In fact this is not true. Three cases can be envisaged:

(1) The government makes a payment by using liquidity originating from the tax yield or from the issue of new securities. In this case, the only consequence of the payment made by the government is to bring back to the private sector liquidity already in possession of the private sector. Therefore we are once more in a situation similar to the one previously examined when the government sector was supposed to be absent.

(2) The payment is made by means of newly created liquidity. In this case, if the government is able to make a payment, this is due to the fact that the banking system, and in this case probably the central bank, has granted a loan to the Treasury.

Once more the payment and the consequent new deposit have been made possible by an initial loan.

(3) A final possible case can be considered if the payment is made not by means of central-bank money but by means of legal tender (coins or notes) issued by the Treasury. In this case, the government takes advantage of its own seigniorage privileges, as though it had granted a loan to itself in order to make the required payments.

The same kind of reasoning can be applied to voluntary or compulsory reserves held by commercial banks against deposits. Reserves in possession of commercial banks also originate from a previous loan made by the banking system. In this case, the loan is granted by the central bank, be it in favour of the banks or in favour of the government. The government borrows reserves in order to make payments to single agents, who subsequently pay the sums into a bank deposit. In both cases, banks draw their reserves from a previous loan granted by the central bank.

## 4.2  Tobin's critique

The priority of loans over deposits was criticised by James Tobin in a famous article of 1963. Tobin's demonstration was based on a simple reasoning. If a bank deposit has to be in existence, there must be an agent wishing to hold it. Therefore, in Tobin's view, the basic element for the existence of bank deposits is not the decision of a bank to grant a loan, but the decision taken by one or more agents to hold a part of their wealth in the form of a bank deposit. If all agents should decide to keep their own wealth in a different form (real goods, gold bars, jewels, securities), bank deposits would necessarily disappear. After all, what determines the existence of bank deposits is not the presence of bank loans but the existence of a demand for deposits. In Tobin's view, the volume of bank deposits depends on the decisions of savers concerning the composition of their portfolio (Tobin 1963).

In formulating his interpretation, Tobin was reverting to some basic elements of Keynesian theory, namely:

- that the demand for money is a demand for a liquid balance to be held against possible contingencies and therefore is a demand for a specific kind of wealth;
- that the same demand depends on how agents decide to allocate their wealth between money and interest-bearing securities;
- that this decision, coupled with the existing stock of money, sets the level of the interest rate.

However, since Keynes in his *General Theory* considers money in general and pays no specific attention to the creation of bank deposits, Tobin's interpretation, which analyses the creation of bank money, should be considered an integration, more than an interpretation, of the Keynesian construction. In fact, Tobin's approach was considered deeply innovative. While in the traditional view of banking (as already noted in §2.7), bank loans are determined by the amount of savings, in Tobin's reformulation the ultimate factor is not saving but the portfolio choices of the agents, and therefore the way in which agents decide to allocate their savings among real goods, securities and bank deposits.

However, Tobin's innovation is not wholly convincing. There is no question about the fact that agents take decisions concerning the composition of their own wealth. But the mere fact that an agent can take decisions concerning the structure of his portfolio does not imply that his decisions have the power of increasing or reducing the total amount of bank deposits.

In order to examine this point, let us consider the case of an agent wanting to alter the composition of his own portfolio. If he intends to increase his bank deposits, he must sell some other asset (real goods or securities); if he intends to reduce them, he will use part of his bank deposits to buy a different kind of asset. In both cases, he can carry out this plan if and only if he finds at least one other agent wanting to alter his portfolio in the opposite direction. The net result of the whole operation is that the total amount of bank deposits remains unchanged.

If we now raise the opposite question, namely what kind of operation might produce an increase or a decrease in the total amount of deposits, the answer will be a totally different one. The only operation producing an increase in the total amount of bank deposits is the decision of a bank to grant a new loan. Similarly, a decrease in total deposits can only be obtained if an agent makes use of a deposit in order to reduce his bank debt. It is, however, clear that the decision to reduce an agent's bank debt produces as a consequence a decrease in the amount of a bank loan. The conclusion is that the only way of altering the total amount of deposits is by altering the total amount of bank loans.

Let us now consider an economy having two means of payment, namely bank deposits and legal tender, and let us consider the case of an agent wanting to decrease his bank deposit in order to increase his holdings of legal tender. It is well known that any increase in the preference for cash decreases the credit potential of the banking system. If the banks were initially loaned up, they are forced to decrease their loans and consequently their deposits. But this is connected with the existence of a compulsory reserve and is not a consequence of a fall in the demand for bank deposits.

Finally we can examine a last possible case. Let us imagine that savers' preference for bank deposits increases. The flow of savings is now directed in a greater proportion to deposits and in a smaller proportion to securities. The result is that firms are forced to ask for higher loans and their bank debt increases. It may seem that the amount of loans has increased as a consequence of an increase in the demand for deposits; in fact it has increased as a consequence of a higher demand for loans, not of a higher supply and even less as a consequence of more credit being made available by the banks.

The idea that deposits make loans is still so widespread because most authors consider in the first place the case of one single isolated bank trying to attract reserves by means of attracting deposits. While it is undeniable that an increase in deposits, by increasing the amount of reserves, adds to the credit potential of a single bank, the same conclusion cannot be applied to the banking system as a whole, since the reserves of the whole banking system can only increase as a consequence of an increase in loans granted by the central bank, either to single banks or to the government. It seems therefore that the principle that loans make deposits should not be abandoned.

## 4.3   A comment on the literature

It cannot be ignored that, while the principle that loans make deposits is widely accepted as a general rule, still the opposite principle, that deposits make loans, often peeps out here and there in the literature. The typically neoclassical underlying idea is that, savings being a prerequisite for investment and bank deposits being a form of saving, the role of deposits is one of channelling liquidity to investors. As already explained, the persistent idea of the priority of savings over investment might find an explanation in the fact that, in an economy in which *real wages are paid in advance*, savings actually do precede investment (§2.3; see also Graziani 1994). But the neoclassical model is based on the opposite idea, namely that wages, along with any other form of income, are paid at the end of the productive process. In this case, the necessity of a prior supply of saving disappears. A remnant of the older theory of wages, although unjustified, seems to survive in present-day banking theory.

A typical instance of this mental attitude can be found in the literature on asymmetric information. It is often maintained that, because of a lack of information concerning single investors, savers may avoid direct loans and prefer to leave their savings in bank deposits. Such savings, however, are not subtracted from investment since the banks, thanks to the larger amount of deposits they collect, are able to grant a greater volume of loans. Unfortunately, as already noted, this reasoning is not correct. If a saver has some liquidity available, its origins can only be one the following: (a) if the liquidity originates from the banking sector, the fact of holding it in the form of a bank deposit adds nothing to the credit potential of the banking system as a whole; (b) if it originates from government deficit spending, it does add to the potential credit of the banking system. But this is due to the presence of deficit spending that originates from a debt of the government to the central bank, which means that the increase it produces in bank deposits is due to a previous loan (precisely, the loan granted by the central bank to the government). Finally, (c) if a saver decides to grant a personal loan to another agent, his decision, while decreasing his own deposit and increasing the deposit of someone else, leaves the total amount of deposits unaltered. In any case, a loan is the inescapable root of any deposit.

## 4.4   The credit potential of a single bank

The analysis of the credit potential of the banking system as a whole is nowadays a consolidated aspect of banking theory. The credit potential of a single bank is a far less explored matter. We shall briefly touch on the second problem and dwell longer on the first one.

If a compulsory reserve ratio prevails, the credit potential of *the banking system as a whole* depends on the monetary base, the compulsory reserve ratio and the preference of the public for cash over deposits. If $r$ is the compulsory reserve ratio, $c$ the fraction of total liquid holdings (cash plus bank deposits) that agents want to hold in the form of cash, $Z$ the total amount of cash in circulation, partly held by the banks ($Z_B$), partly by the public ($Z_P$), $D$ bank deposits and $CR$ total credit (cash in the hands of the public plus bank deposits), the structural equations, expressing in symbols the definitions just given, are:

$$Z = Z_B + Z_P$$
$$Z_B = rD$$
$$CR = Z_P + D$$
$$Z_P = c(Z_P + D).$$

By substitution we get the definition of bank deposits:

$$D = \frac{1 - c}{c + r(1 - c)} Z$$

If a compulsory reserve is absent ($r = 0$), the formula reduces to:

$$D = \frac{1 - c}{c} Z.$$

In a hypothetical pure credit system, where all exchanges are regulated by transferring bank deposits and legal tender is not required ($c = 0$), the credit potential of the banking system becomes unlimited ($D$ tends to infinity as $c$ tends to zero). In the absence of a compulsory reserve ratio and with a zero preference for cash, the system of commercial banks meets no limits in the expansion of credit. The same result for the banking system as a whole (central bank plus commercial banks) prevails in a closed economy free from the need of holding reserves in foreign currencies. As the banker and economist L.A. Hahn once said, one needs to subtract cash out of bank deposits and take it to the moon in order to create liquidity problems for the banking system as a whole (Hahn, 1954; also Hahn 1920). The same principle can be applied to all the national banking systems, which means that the world banking system as a whole meets no limits in its capacity for credit creation. The banking system of one single country enjoys the same principle provided it expands credit in step with other countries (the same is true of any single bank, provided it expands its own credit in parallel with other banks, Keynes 1971 [1930], vol. I, chapter 2, §i: 26).

Let us now consider the case of one single bank. Similar to what is true of the banking system as a whole, the credit potential of a single bank depends on the amount of available reserves, on the compulsory reserve ratio, if present, on the preferences of the public for cash over deposits and for deposits of the same bank over deposits of other banks. Each one of these factors deserves separate examination.

The amount of reserves at the disposal of a single bank depends on the total amount of reserves created by the central bank and on the fraction of total reserves that the single bank succeeds in securing for itself. The amount of reserves of a single bank depends therefore on its ability to attract new customers; that's why a competition develops among single banks, each one of them trying to attract the highest fraction of the market and therefore of reserves created by the central bank.

Something similar holds concerning the preference for deposits of a particular bank over cash or over deposits with other banks. Each bank tries to increase the number of its own customers because an increase in the share of the deposit market produces two positive effects: it increases the amount of reserves collected by the bank while at the same time decreasing, as we shall presently see, the reserve requirements of that bank. The credit potential of the bank is thereby doubly increased.

While the compulsory reserve ratio is obviously the same for each bank belonging to the same country, the voluntary reserve is determined by each bank on the basis of its own management criteria. In brief, the reserve requirements of each bank are inversely related to the market share of the bank in the market for deposits.

In order to make this last point clear, we can argue as follows. An imaginary bank, serving the whole of the market, needs no reserves: exactly as the banking system considered in its entirety, its credit potential would be unlimited and it would be able to grant any amount of loans at its own discretion. This hypothetical case evokes the famous image due to Irving Fisher of money created 'by the stroke of a pen'. At the other extreme, an equally imaginary bank having one customer only would be forced to hold an amount of reserves equal to the amount of deposits collected: in fact any loan granted to its only customer implies by definition an equal loss of reserves as soon as the beneficiary of the loan makes use of it by making a payment. Its credit potential would be identical to the amount of reserves in its possession.

When, as is usually the case, the bank has a percentage share of the market between 0 and 100, its reserve requirement will be lower the higher its share of the market. This point was made by Wicksell when he observed that a bank occupying the whole market for deposits would enjoy the same unlimited credit potential as the banking system as a whole (Wicksell (1936 [1898]), chapter 6, section C: 66–8). The same point, even if with a somewhat incomplete presentation, was made by Edgeworth in his essay on the mathematical theory of the bank. Edgeworth's model doesn't include the market share of a bank as a variable. Edgeworth considers instead the specific case of n banks deciding to set up a mutual coordination mechanism by keeping their own reserves in one main bank, and remarks that in this case 'the average reserve which is now necessary will be less than n times the previous average reserve' (Edgeworth 1888: 126). A number of banks pooling their own reserves are very similar to one single bigger bank; Edgeworth's example is therefore totally parallel to the case now being considered. A divergence between the two cases exists only in that Edgeworth, just as the majority of other authors, only considers the danger of customers withdrawing liquidity from a bank in order to hold it as cash while neglecting the possibility of a bank losing liquidity because some of its customers move deposits to another bank. If we consider both possibilities, it will be clear that two parameters are involved, the preference of the public for cash and the market share of the single bank considered. As remarked above, each bank has therefore a double reason for constantly trying to subtract deposits from other banks: each increase in its own deposits not only increases the absolute amount of its own reserves but also decreases the level of the required reserve ratio.

In more formal terms, let us imagine a market where $N$ agents are present, each of them making the same amount of payments per unit of time. If $N_j$ is the number of depositors of bank $j$, the market share $d_j$ of the same bank will be:

$$d_j = \frac{N_j}{N}.$$

The probability that any agent may make a payment to a customer of a different bank, thus causing a loss of reserves to bank $j$, will be:

$$p_1 = \frac{N - N_j}{N - 1} = \frac{1 - d_j}{1 - 1/N}.$$

If a bank succeeds in keeping stable its own market share (which means that $N$ and $N_j$ move in proportion) we can say that the value of $p_1$ tends to $1 - d_j$ as $N$ tends to infinity.

Let us define $\varphi$ as the probability that, within a given period assumed as one unit of accounting, any payment made to a customer of another bank is not compensated within the same time period by a corresponding and equal payment in the opposite direction. The probability that a bank will suffer a loss of liquidity equals the composite probability of the two events: (a) that one of its own customers makes a payment to a customer of a different bank; and (b) that, within the same time period, this payment is not compensated by a simultaneous payment in the opposite direction. Such probability, for $N$ tending to infinity, is:

$$p_2 = (1 - d_j)\varphi.$$

Let us assume that the reserve ratio considered as optimal by the bank is proportional to the probability of suffering a loss of reserves with a coefficient equal to $\theta$ reflecting the attitude of the bank towards risk. The optimal reserve ratio $r^*$ will be:

$$r^* = \theta(1 - d_j)\varphi. \tag{4.1}$$

We can now revert to the credit potential of the single bank. The potential amount of deposits of one single bank, $D_j$, equals the volume of reserves $Z_j$ multiplied by the inverse of the reserve ratio:

$$D_j = \frac{1}{\theta(1 - d_j)\varphi} Z_j.$$

The fraction of total reserves in existence, $Z$, in possession of the bank can be defined as equal to the market share of the bank in the deposit market: $Z_j = d_j Z$. Consequently we can write:

$$D_j = \frac{d_j}{\theta(1 - d_j)\varphi} Z. \tag{4.2}$$

If no government sector is present and all reserves in possession of commercial banks are borrowed reserves, and if loans to private agents are the only assets of commercial banks, loans equal deposits and the preceding formula is also a measure of the credit potential of each single bank.

If a government sector is present and getting credit from the central bank, the sum total of reserves equals the sum of the debts of commercial banks plus the debt of the government to the central bank:

$$Z = Z_B + Z_G.$$

The budget constraint of a single commercial bank requires that assets (loans $L_j$ plus reserves $Z_j$) be equal to liabilities (deposits $D_j$ plus debts towards the central bank $Z_{Bj}$):

$$L_j = D_j + Z_{Bj} - Z_j.$$

By substituting the last definition of reserves and remembering that the reserves of one single bank equal the fraction

$d_j$ of total reserves $(Z_j = d_j Z)$, we get:

$$L_j = D_j + d_j Z_B - d_j(Z_B + Z_G)$$

and:

$$L_j = D_j - d_j Z_G.$$

Substituting the definition of deposits (4.2) gives:

$$L_j = \frac{d_j}{\theta(1 - d_j)\varphi} Z - d_j Z_G.$$

Since: $Z = Z_B + Z_G$, we get:

$$L_j = d_j \left[ \left( \frac{1}{\theta(1 - d_j)\varphi} - 1 \right) + \frac{1}{\theta(1 - d_j)\varphi} Z_B \right].$$

As can be seen, the capacity of each single bank to create credit depends not only on the amount of total reserves but also on the share of the bank in the market for deposits.

It should be added that a substantially similar analysis is contained in Tobin's model of the banking firm (Tobin 1982a). Tobin does not mention the market share of a single bank, and introduces instead a variable denominated *rate of re-depositing* indicating the measure in which loans granted by one single bank are used to make payments to customers of the same bank, thus avoiding any loss of reserves. The rate of re-depositing is clearly different as compared to the market share of a bank. Still it can be used to analyse the same phenomenon, since the higher the market share of a bank the higher the probability that loans granted by the bank will be used to make payments to customers of the same bank.[3]

---

[3] Tobin's analysis contains one obscure point. In defining the deposits of a single bank, Tobin includes an autonomous element $D_o$, the nature of which remains unexplained. Since the whole of deposits is created by the whole of loans, the sum total of the $D_{oj}$ terms appearing in the deposits of the single banks should equal zero. Alternatively, if we limit our consideration to the set of commercial banks, omitting the central bank and the government sector, the sum total of the $D_{oj}$ terms should equal the monetary base created by the government deficit, this being the amount of deposits that commercial banks can collect without having themselves granted any previous loan.

The preceding result, by connecting the credit potential of one single bank to its market share, explains why bankers insist on the idea that only by collecting deposits are they enabled to grant loans. It would be more correct to say that, while a single bank could grant credit without having previously collected a deposit and without having borrowed the required reserves from the central bank, still it is clear that collecting deposits increases in more than one way the credit potential of the single bank. At the same time, the same idea is clearly wrong if applied to the banking system as a whole. Here the opposite principle is true, namely that loans create deposits. The priority of deposits over loans could be true only if the analysis were limited to the sector of commercial banks, excluding the central bank, and assuming that the government deficit is the only source of reserves, since in this case, collecting deposits would be the only way open for commercial banks to capture reserves.

# 5

# The distribution of income

## 5.1 Theories of income distribution

At least three different basic models of income formation and distribution can be distinguished.

The first is part of the more traditional neoclassical theory, based on autonomous choices of single agents. Negotiations in the labour market equalise for each individual the marginal utility of goods and the marginal disutility of labour. An equilibrium level of employment (number of employed and duration of work) is thus determined. The level of employment, coupled with the endowment of productive resources and available technologies, determines aggregate product and therefore, in a closed economy, national income. At the same time, once given the level of employment, the marginal product of labour is also determined, and therefore the level of real wages and the distribution of income between wages and profits. The preferences of consumers, within the constraints of factor endowments and technological knowledge, thus determine the general equilibrium of the whole economic system. As already noted, followers of the circulation approach reject the basic idea of consumer sovereignty in favour, as we shall presently see, of the opposite idea of producer sovereignty.

A second formulation is the one adopted by Keynes in his *General Theory*. Here national income is no longer determined by the individual choices of consumers but by the joint action of investment, decided by producers, on the one side, and of consumers' propensity to save through the multiplier mechanism on the other. Once the level of income is determined, income distribution follows the marginal rule (it is a well-known fact that, in the *General Theory*, Keynes accepts what he calls the first postulate of the classical theory, namely the equality between the real wage rate and the marginal product of labour, Keynes 1973a [1936], chapter 2).

A third formulation, adopted by Keynes himself in *A Treatise on Money* (1971 [1930]), was subsequently reformulated by Nicholas Kaldor and Joan Robinson, and is now commonly known as the post-Keynesian theory of income distribution.[1] Here firms decide in full autonomy the level of production and the allocation of resources between production of consumer goods and capital goods (or alternatively: entrepreneurs decide the level of investment, while the production of consumer goods is determined as a residual, since full employment is assumed to prevail, and aggregate product is determined by the amount of available resources). Since the two different propensities to consume of capitalists and wage earners are given, the distribution of income between wages and profits must be such as to determine an equality between demand and supply on the market for commodities, and therefore an equilibrium between investment and saving.

A variant of the so-called post-Keynesian model was formulated by Kalecki (1990 [1933], 1991 [1942]). In his model, entrepreneurs enjoy a monopoly position on the commodities market. They are therefore able to set the price–cost ratio, their own profit margin and therefore the distribution of income between wages and profits. Since the propensities to consume of capitalists and wage earners are given,

---

[1] Kaldor 1956. A detailed overview of post-Keynesian theory is contained in Arestis 1997, chapters 4 and 5.

the distribution of income determines the average propensity to consume and the value of the income multiplier. The multiplier, coupled to the volume of investments decided by entrepreneurs, determines the level of aggregate income. In substance the Kaleckian version does not differ from the post-Keynesian construction. If entrepreneurs offer for sale given amounts of consumer goods and capital goods, leaving the determination of prices to market forces, the result is substantially equivalent to the case in which entrepreneurs set the price of consumer goods at a level that makes the quantity demanded equal to the amount that entrepreneurs have decided to sell.

As already said, followers of the circulation approach reject the neoclassical theory of employment and distribution and follow the so-called Keynes–Kalecki formulation, a formulation corresponding closely to the post-Keynesian theory of Kaldor and Robinson.

## 5.2   Different purchasing power

The basic assumption of the circulation approach concerning income distribution is that wage earners and firms enjoy widely differing purchasing power over commodities in the market. The expenditure of wage earners is strictly limited by the budget constraint set by the wage bill, while the position of firms is totally different.

In the market for resources firms, by using the bank credit granted to them, hire labour according to their own production plans. The same firms enter the market for finished products, where a multiplicity of exchanges take place, both between firms and consumers and among single firms. By way of such exchanges within the firm sector, each firm acquires the fraction of total product required for further production. The nature of such exchanges among firms can be interpreted in different ways. Some authors, by applying a rigorous logical reasoning, respect the initial assumption according to which the firms sector has been defined as one single integrated and consolidated sector. Given this approach, they prefer to ignore the presence of firms in the market for finished products, since this would imply that one and the same agent is selling and buying the product that he himself has produced. Once the firms sector has been defined as being integrated into one single agent, it seems more logical to imagine that firms do not put on sale the fraction of total product that they plan to use in their own production.

A similar solution, while being fully consistent with the structure of the model, omits at least one relevant aspect of the process, namely the way in which purchases made by firms in the commodity market are financed. In order to avoid neglecting this point, it seems advisable to abandon the initial definition of the firm sector as one that is fully integrated and revert to the more realistic image of a multiplicity of firms, not only selling goods to consumers but also exchanging finished products among themselves. In order to avoid analytical complications, let us keep the assumption of one single product, to be used both for consumption and as a means of production. This allows us to examine how firms' purchases of finished goods are financed, a point not to be neglected in the general framework of the circulation approach.

In order to buy finished goods, firms need finance as much as they need finance for paying the wage bill in the labour market. Two kinds of demand are now present in the market for finished goods, the demand of wage earners, limited to the wage bill, and the demand coming from the firms, limited only by the credit they can get from the banks. The amount of finance the firms need equals the quantity of finished goods to be purchased multiplied by the price prevailing on the market.

It is easy to see that, in principle, firms can get from the banks (and the banks are willing to grant them) any amount of finance, no matter how great. In fact, the finance granted by banks and used by firms for making purchases in the commodity market, while being a debt to some of the firms, will be revenue to others. If we consider a closed economy and ignore the possibility of an increase in liquid holdings, finance will move from one firm to another without ever leaving the firm sector. Therefore firms as a whole will never have problems in repaying their bank debt. Whatever the initial loan may have been, firms as a whole will be able to repay it. As for the banking sector, a parallel situation prevails. It may well be that a loan granted to one single firm is not repaid, which means that there may be one single bank having liquidity problems. But, considering the banking sector in its entirety, if one bank is short of liquidity, there will be other banks having an excess liquidity, and the sector as a whole will experience no loss of reserves.

As a consequence it can be assumed that, so long as the possibility of an increase in hoarding is ruled out, firms will have no problems in getting whatever amount of finance they need. The possibility of getting any amount of finance endows firms with purchasing power which is in principle unlimited.

## 5.3　The formation of money prices

Let us adopt the following notation:

$w$ = money wage rate

$N$ = total employment

$c, s$ = propensities to consume and to save of wage earners

$b$ = fraction of aggregate product that firms decide to acquire for their own use (or real investment)

$\pi$ = average productivity of labour

$X$ = amount of finished product (consumption plus investment)

$C$ = aggregate consumption

$I$ = aggregate real investment

$I_m$ = aggregate monetary investment

$B$ = total amount outstanding of securities issued by the firms

$i$ = percentage yield of securities

$p$ = market price of the finished product.

Interest payments made in each period by firms to savers, equal to $iB$, must be added to income from labour in order to get the total income of wage earners.

Aggregate supply is equal to:

$$X = \pi N.$$

Aggregate demand in the commodities market equals consumption plus investment. Consumption of wage earners is equal to:

$$C = c(wN + iB).$$

Firms offer for sale the whole of the finished product. At the same time they enter the market as buyers having decided to buy the fraction $b$ of aggregate product. In monetary terms their investment expenditure is:

$$I = b\pi Np.$$

The equilibrium price level is determined by the equality between demand and supply:

$$\pi Np = c(wN + iB) + b\pi Np,$$

which gives for the equilibrium price:

$$p = \frac{1-s}{1-b}\left[\frac{w}{\pi} + \frac{iB}{\pi N}\right].$$

The term in square brackets measures the cost of production in monetary terms (wages plus interest costs per unit of product), while the factor $(1 - s)/(1 - b)$ is a multiplier allowing the move from costs to prices, and is therefore a measure of the profit margin.

The preceding result suggests the following:

a)   Money prices do not depend on the quantity of money: in fact the money stock does not even appear in the price equation (being a totally endogenous variable, the money stock cannot appear as a variable determining prices).

b)   The price level depends instead on the propensities to save and to invest and on the level of money costs (money wages and the interest rate paid on securities).

c)   Each variation in the price level produces a proportional variation in the money stock, so far as the velocity of circulation is assumed to be constant.

The average real income of wage earners is:

$$\frac{w + i(B/N)}{p} = \frac{w + i(B/N)}{\dfrac{1-s}{1-b}\left(\dfrac{w}{\pi} + \dfrac{iB}{\pi N}\right)} = \frac{1-b}{1-s}\pi.$$

Real consumption per worker is equal to:

$$c\frac{1-b}{1-s} = (1-b)\pi.$$

The preceding result warrants a comment. Average real consumption of wage earners depends not only on the average productivity of labour but also on the share $b$ of total product that firms decide to buy for themselves in order to use in further production (investment). It does not depend instead, as one might reasonably think, on the absolute number employed in the consumer goods sector. This means that, on its own, an increase in the absolute production of consumer goods is not sufficient for wage earners to obtain an increase in per capita real consumption: it is also necessary for firms to reduce the share of aggregate product they decide to buy. In order to obtain an increase in real consumption per capita, wage earners need not only an increase in the amount produced of consumer goods but also an alteration in the structure of employment, with a lower share of workers employed in the production of investment goods.

The *rate of profit* can be defined as the ratio between the value of net aggregate product and the monetary cost of production:

$$r = \frac{\pi Np - (wN + iB)}{wN + iB} = \frac{1-s}{1-b} - 1 = \frac{b-s}{1-b}.$$

Total profits in monetary terms are defined as the profit rate times the monetary value of capital invested:

$$P = r(wN + iB) = \frac{b-s}{1-b}(wN + iB).$$

Profits in real terms are equal to money profits divided by the price level:

$$P/p = \frac{\dfrac{b-s}{1-b}(wN + iB)}{\dfrac{1-s}{1-b}\left(\dfrac{w}{\pi} + \dfrac{iB}{\pi N}\right)} = \frac{b-s}{1-s}\pi N.$$

The preceding result requires the following comments:

a)   The level of profits depends directly on the level of money prices. As Bernard Schmitt, one of the founders of the circulation approach, would say: 'profits are born in the commodities market' (Schmitt 1984, chapter 4: 134–5).

b)   Real profits do not depend on the interest rate paid by firms on the securities they issue. A consequence is that any attempt to influence investment decisions by controlling the rate of interest is bound to be ineffective since it doesn't affect firms' profits. This is also true of interest paid by firms to savers on securities issued by the firms themselves, although not of interest paid by firms to the banks, since in this case a transfer of real wealth from industry to finance occurs.

c)   If $s = b$, namely if, by chance, the propensities to save and to invest, in spite of their being connected to totally independent social groups, happen to be equal, the expression for money prices reduces to:

$$p = \frac{w}{\pi} + \frac{iB}{\pi N}.$$

In this special case, prices equal the monetary cost of production while profits, beyond the normal remuneration of the entrepreneur already included in the cost as the reward for a special kind of labour, are absent. The equilibrium in this case is altogether similar to an equilibrium of perfect competition.

d)   If $s = 0$, that is if wage earners consume the whole of their income, real profits become $P/p = b\pi N$ and, clearly, profits equal investment. Since investment, as noted before, corresponds to the expenditure of capitalists, in this case the famous conclusion reached by Kalecki, that while wage earners spend what they earn *capitalists earn what they spend*, emerges as literally correct (Kalecki 1990 [1933]).

The profits discussed up to now are those earned before interest is paid to the banks. In order to calculate net profit, the interest burden on the current bank debt must be subtracted. As already said, in our simplified case, the bank debt of the firms equals the liquid balances of savers. We can assume liquid balances to be a fraction $L$ of current income, the fraction being inversely related to the rate of interest paid by the firms on securities. We get, therefore:

$$L = L(i) \, (wN + iB).$$

The interest burden of the firms towards the banks equals this sum multiplied by the interest rate paid to the banks. Net profits therefore will be:

$$P_n = r(wN + iB) - i_{BK}[L(i)(wN + iB)].$$

The preceding expression makes it clear that an increase in the interest rate paid by firms on securities produces contrasting consequences. Let us assume, to begin with, that while bank interest rate remains constant, firms increase the interest they pay on securities. The increase in the yield from securities produces a decrease in the speculative demand for money, $L(i)$. At the same time, the income of savers is increased, which produces an increase in the transactions demand for liquid balances. The net result depends on the relative weights of the two reactions. If an increase in the rate of interest paid on securities is accompanied by a parallel increase in the rate paid to the banks, the probability that an increase in the structure of interest rates will reduce profits will be higher (on this specific problem more will be added in §6.1).

## 5.4  Government expenditure and the tax yield

The preceding results are not greatly altered if the government sector is present. This case can be briefly commented on as follows.

As already noted, so far as the demand for money is constant, we can assume that firms enjoy unlimited access to bank credit for their purchases in the commodities market, for the dual reasons that firms as a whole have no problems in repaying their bank debt and consequently the banks, again taken as a whole, are prepared to grant them any amount of loans. This means that, irrespective of the level of their tax liability, firms will always be able to buy what they desire in the commodities market. Taxes levied on firms therefore give rise to a purely nominal burden which has no consequence in real terms. Even in the extreme case in which taxes on firms are 100 per cent and the tax yield is spent entirely on subsidies to wage earners, the real position of firms will not be affected.

The case of wage earners is obviously different. Wage earners can only spend within the budget constraint set by the wage bill. When purchasing finished goods in the commodity market they are bound to be defeated by the competition of firms. As a consequence, wage earners can buy only those finished products which remain in the market after the firms have bought what they have planned to acquire for themselves. The situation can in no way be modified by introducing subsidies in favour of consumers. Unless firms alter their own plans, subsidies cannot increase the real consumption of wage earners, their only effect being to increase in proportion both the nominal income of wage earners and the level of money prices.

If the government, instead of assigning subsidies to wage earners, makes use of the tax yield to buy finished goods directly, the result is that the government, wage earners and firms compete in the commodities market. The firms, thanks to the possibility of unlimited recourse to bank credit, are sure to realise their own plans, so their profits are untouched in real terms. The government also will realise its plans in real terms to a greater or lesser extent according to whether government expenditure has been set in money or in real terms. Wage earners are most probably those who will see their consumption reduced in real terms. It must be concluded, as Kalecki did, that, in spite of taxes being levied on profits, firms do not pay any tax in real terms. The only ones to pay taxes in real terms are wage earners (Kalecki 1990 [1933] and 1991 [1942]; similar remarks are to be found in Keynes 1971 [1930], vol. 1: 298ff.).

In more formal terms, the situation can be described as follows:

*Case 1*: Consider a case in which government expenditure is totally financed by means of deficit spending. This is tantamount to saying that the government goes into debt with the central bank for the whole amount of its expenditure. Let us also assume that government expenditure is totally used for paying subsidies to wage earners, the amount of total subsidies being set as a fraction of the total income of wage earners.

Government expenditure $G$ can be defined as the fraction $g$ of income of wage earners:

$$G = g(wN + iB).$$

Let us assume the amount of securities in existence to be given and that each wage earner owns on average an amount of securities equal to $\alpha$. We get:

$$\alpha = B/N$$

and:

$$G = g(w + \alpha i)N.$$

The price level will be:

$$p = (1 + g)\left(\frac{1 - s}{1 - b}\right)\left(\frac{w + i\alpha}{\pi}\right).$$

The preceding expression makes it clear that, as already noticed, money prices do not depend on the quantity of money, which is an endogenous variable. Money prices do not depend either, at least not in any direct way, on how government expenditure is financed. Government expenditure may certainly have inflationary consequences; but such consequences are not produced by the increase in the stock of money, but only indirectly by the increase in aggregate demand. Moreover, in contrast to what is often believed, the inflationary effects are higher the more government expenditure is financed by issuing government bonds, since in that case the increase in the stock of government bonds in existence brings about an increase in the value of $\alpha$ and in the level of money prices (a similar result was obtained by Blinder and Solow, 1974: 48ff.).

The rate of profit, defined as before as the value of net aggregate product divided by the money cost of production, is now equal to:

$$r = (1 + g)\frac{b - s}{1 - b}$$

and total profits, defined as before as the value of invested capital times the rate of profit, are equal to:

$$P = (1 + g)\frac{b - s}{1 - b}(wN + iB).$$

It emerges clearly that any increase in the price level produced by government expenditure will produce an increase in money profits. However, real profits are unchanged, since money profits and money prices increase by the same proportion $(1 + g)$. Thus, it can be concluded that a government expenditure entirely financed by creation of money and entirely used for paying subsidies to wage earners brings about a redistribution of real consumption inside the group of wage earners, in favour of those who get the subsidies and against those who don't, while leaving real profits unchanged.

Let us now consider profits net of financial burdens. The situation is now different. Net money profits are equal to:

$$P_n = (1 + g)\frac{b - s}{1 - b}(wN + iB) - i_{BK}[L(i)(wN + iB)]$$

$$= \left[(1 + g)\frac{b - s}{1 - b} - i_{BK}L(i)\right](wN + iB).$$

Net profits, equal to money profits divided by the price level, are now equal to:

$$P_n/p = \pi N\left(\frac{b - s}{1 - s} - \frac{L(i)i_{BK}}{(1 + g)(1 - s)/(1 - b)}\right).$$

While real gross profits are unchanged even in the presence of government expenditure and inflation, real net profits are increased, since inflation decreases the financial burden of firms. In fact, when the government pays subsidies by means of deficit spending, the firms get higher receipts from selling their products. Since the initial expenditure for hiring labour and the connected interest burden are unchanged, the interest burden in real terms is now lower, which means higher real profits. In this case, government expenditure redistributes income in favour of profits and against the banking sector.

*Case 2*: Let us now consider a second case, in which government expenditure is financed by the tax yield so that the government budget is balanced. Let us also assume that the expenditure is not used to pay subsidies but to buy finished goods.

Let us assume a tax levied proportionally on all kinds of income (wages and profits). To make the reasoning simpler let us neglect income from capital of savers, namely the $iB$ component. Let $t$ be the tax rate common to all taxpayers. The tax yield, equal to government expenditure, will be:

$$T = G = twN + t(\pi Np - wN).$$

The expenditure of wage earners in the commodities market is now reduced by a fraction $t$. The expenditure of firms is unchanged since firms enjoy unlimited purchasing power in the commodities market. The equality between demand and supply now is:

$$\pi Np = (1 - t)\, cwN + b\pi Np + t\pi Np,$$

and we get for the price level:

$$p = \frac{(1 - t)(1 - s)}{1 - b - t}\, \frac{w}{\pi}.$$

The firms' profits after tax are:

$$P = (1 - t)(\pi Np - wN).$$

By substituting the price equation we get:

$$P = (1 - t)\, \frac{b - s(1 - t)}{1 - b - t}\, wN.$$

Real profits are equal to:

$$P/p = \frac{b - s(1 - t)}{1 - s}\, \pi N.$$

The result is that the presence of taxes increases profits. The logic is that the payment of taxes forces wage earners to reduce their propensity to save out of income before taxes (even if the propensity to save out of income after taxes is unchanged). Investment by firms as a fraction of income is unchanged, but a higher proportion is acquired by firms as profits and a lower proportion is available to wage earners for investing in securities.

If we now consider profits after paying interest to the banks, we get a similar result. Net profits are equal to:

$$P_n = \left[ (1 - t) \frac{b - s(1 - t)}{1 - b - t} - i_{BK} L(i) \right] wN.$$

In real terms we get:

$$P_n / p = \left[ \frac{b - s(1 - t)}{1 - s} - \frac{(1 - t)(1 - s)}{1 - b - t} i_{BK} L(i) \right] wN.$$

Also in this case real net profits are increased by the presence of taxes.

## 5.5  Productive and unproductive sectors

Retail trade is often criticised as an inefficient sector occupying an exceedingly high number of employees having low productivity. Not all scholars agree with this interpretation. Some maintain that the retail trade sector in itself increases consumers' welfare in that it provides a better spatial distribution of the product, thus allowing economies in time and transportation costs. In a totally contrasting perspective, others say that consumer satisfaction depends only on the technical qualities of the product, and is independent of both its location and any complementary services that the retail trade can provide. In this latter view, any increase in employment in the retail sector is considered as detrimental to consumers' welfare, since it subtracts resources from the manufacturing sector, thereby reducing the total amount of available commodities.

The conception of retail trade as a fully productive activity earning a rate of profit equal to that of any other sector goes back to Adam Smith (1993 [1776], book II, chapter 5). The opposite conception is to be found in Sismondi who considered trade incapable of increasing the value of production. In his view, the presence of retail trade has the consequence only of redistributing an unchanged profit among three different groups of agents, producers, wholesale traders and retail traders (Sismondi 1991 [1819], book II, chapter 8).

The two contrasting visions bring about analytical considerations equally different. If trade is considered as a productive sector, the equilibrium position is defined according to the usual competitive conditions: employment in trade (or in the tertiary sector in general) has to be such as to make the productivity of labour equal to the real wage and the rate of profit has to be equal to the one prevailing in any other sector. If instead trade is viewed as an unproductive activity, the level of employment cannot be connected to any productivity consideration. Those who follow a similar interpretation consider employment in the trade sector as uniquely determined by the number of labourers being excluded from other sectors. Employment in the trade sector turns out to be a sort of residual variable determining the productivity of labour and consequently the level of the real wage rate, which will inevitably be lower than the one prevailing in the remaining sectors. The result will be a dualistic labour market.

The introduction of the trade sector requires some alterations in the notation so far used. The new notation will be:

$X$ = amount of finished product, to be used both for consumption and for investment

$N$ = total employment

$N^i$ = employment in the industrial sector

$N^t$ = employment in the trade sector

$\sigma$ = fraction of employment in the industrial sector present in the trade sector ($N^t = \sigma N^i$)

$\pi$ = labour productivity in the productive sectors

$p, p^t$ = production and retail prices.

Let us make the following assumptions:

a)    Wage earners spend the whole of their wages on consumer goods $(c = 1, s = 0)$. As a consequence, wage earners own no accumulated wealth and their only income is from labour.

b)    Those employed in the trade sector are self-employed, earning an income equal to the wage prevailing in the productive sectors.

The industrial sector sells its product to the trade sector. The total amount of product delivered to the trade sector and sold to consumers is equal to the quantity that would have been sold to consumers in the absence of a trade sector, namely the whole of production minus the fraction $b$ that the firms have decided to buy for themselves:

$$C = (1 - b)\pi N^i.$$

The price paid by the trade sector is the same as that which would prevail in the absence of commercial intermediation:

$$p = \frac{1}{1-b}\frac{w}{\pi}.$$

Average real consumption is now:

$$\frac{C}{N} = \frac{C}{(1+\sigma)N^i} = \frac{(1-b)\pi N^i}{(1+\sigma)N^i} = \frac{1-b}{1+\sigma}\pi.$$

The trade sector, when selling finished goods, applies a margin high enough to allow its own employees to enjoy an average real consumption equal to the real consumption of productive workers. In order that all employees, both of the productive and of the unproductive sectors, can enjoy the same level of real consumption the available quantity of consumer goods must be distributed as follows:

$$(1 - b)\pi N^i = \frac{1-b}{1+\sigma}\pi N^i + \frac{1-b}{1+\sigma}\pi\sigma N^i,$$

where the first term on the right hand side measures the total amount going to productive workers, the second one the amount going to unproductive workers.

The trade sector sells an amount of consumer goods not greater than the first term (or, as one might say, applies a price margin such as to allow its own employees to purchase an amount not smaller than the second term). The retail price of consumer goods $p^t$ must now satisfy the following equality:

$$\frac{1-b}{1+\sigma}\pi N^i p^t = wN^i$$

$$p^t = \frac{1+\sigma}{1-b}\frac{w}{\pi}.$$

The presence of the trade sector implies therefore *a reduction in the real wage rate of productive workers*. The proportional reduction is equal to the ratio between retail and wholesale prices:

$$p^t/p = 1+\sigma = 1 + N^t/N^i$$

and is therefore higher the greater the fraction of unproductive workers in total employment.

# 6

---

# The role of financial markets

## 6.1 The market for securities

The expenditure by income recipients in the commodities market can be in the nature either of consumption or of real saving (if a saver decides to buy real estate, land, or a house), the remaining part being in the nature of financial saving. In the simplified case we are now considering, financial saving can take only one of two possible forms, either securities (or equities) issued by firms, or holdings of liquidity in the form of bank deposits.

As already made clear, when savers decide to put their current savings into a bank deposit, firms lose the same amount of liquidity and their bank debt is correspondingly increased. The consequence is that banks and firms compete for the available financial savings. In this competition, the banks try to make bank deposits more attractive by paying higher interest rates and by supplying complementary services (or simply, as once remarked by Tobin, by setting up comfortable and well-equipped premises, Tobin 1982a: 498). On the other hand, firms and financial intermediaries, so far as they are concerned, try to attract savings by offering high-yield securities. They also try to stabilise the price of securities on the financial market in order to offer the savers less risky placements. (The crucial role of financial intermediaries is clearly described by Bossone 2001: 878.) Stability over time and yield are in fact the two main features that savers (as distinguished from speculators) evaluate before placing their savings. Whatever the respective features of securities and bank deposits, any agent will usually decide to keep some liquidity in the form of a bank deposit, which automatically creates a debt of the firms towards the banks. The firms have therefore to meet two kinds of financial burden: interest to be paid on securities they themselves have issued and interest to be paid on the bank loans granted to them.

The two kinds of payments take place in two different markets. The first one, interest on securities, takes place in the financial market and is a payment to be made by firms to savers. The second one takes place in the money market and is a payment made by firms to the banks. Different kinds of bonds are typical of the two markets, since short-term bonds are negotiated on the money market, while long-term securities are typical of the financial market. Of course any short-term loan can be rolled over again and again, thus becoming de facto, if both parties agree, a source of long-term finance; but the conditions of the loan can be renegotiated each time, which doesn't happen with long-term securities.

## 6.2  Interest on securities

As previously noted, firms, in order to attract financial saving in the highest possible measure, should increase the yield of the securities they issue. By attracting more financial saving, firms reduce their bank debt while increasing their debt towards savers. The question is now to what extent it pays to do so.

To begin with, let us consider a simplified case in which wage earners make use of their income from capital (namely interest received on securities in their possession) for buying either commodities or securities only, any increase in their holdings of bank deposits being excluded. In this case, firms can pay any amount of interest, no matter how high, without any real cost. In fact, since what the firms pay as interest is again spent either on commodities or on securities, in any case the liquidity flows back to them and they will be able to repay their bank debt. In this respect, the sums paid by firms as interest are similar to the sums paid for wages. Just as with any increase in money wages, any increase in the interest rate paid on securities, while possibly leading to an increase in aggregate demand and, under the usual assumptions of the model, to an increase in prices, implies no additional cost to the firms. If interest paid on securities implies no real cost, firms can set it at any level they like.

The analysis of this simplified case leads to a relevant conclusion typical of the monetary theory of production, namely that monetary payments made to wage earners are never a real cost to firms. The only real costs originate from payments due to the banks.

Apart from the preceding simplified case, it should be remembered that any increase in interest paid on securities, by increasing the income of wage earners, can also bring about an increase in the demand for liquid balances. If the bank deposits of savers increase, the bank debt of firms also increases, giving rise, as we know, to an increase in firms' real costs. As already mentioned (§5.5), an increase in interest rates paid by firms on securities produces therefore a dual effect: (a) an income effect, producing an increase in the demand for liquid balances, which is detrimental to firms; (b) a substitution effect, producing a possible reduction in bank deposits and an increase in the share of wealth held as securities. The second effect is clearly favourable to the firms. We can therefore conclude that for firms an increase in the interest rate paid on deposits is to their advantage whenever the substitution effect prevails over the income effect so that the net outcome is a reduction in bank deposits.

In our simplified case, the financial wealth of any agent is made up of two components: securities issued by the firms,

$B$, and bank deposits, $D$. Bank deposits supply the liquidity needed to cover the interval between payments and receipts. The demand for deposits is a fraction $\mu$ of current income (wages plus interest on securities), inversely related to the rate paid on securities:

$$\mu = \mu(i_b), \quad d\mu/di_B < 0.$$

Assuming interest to be paid at the beginning of each period on securities held at the end of the preceding one, the demand for deposits can be defined as follows:

$$D_d = \mu(i_b)(wN + i_B B).$$

The reaction of the demand for deposits to a change in the yield of securities is:

$$\delta D/\delta i_B = \mu(i_b)B + \delta\mu/\delta i_B(wN + i_B B).$$

The first term corresponds to the income effect measuring the variation in the demand for deposits due to the increase in income. The second term corresponds to the substitution effect, measuring the change in the demand for deposits due to the change in the yield of securities. The first term is surely positive: an increase in the yield of securities, by increasing income, increases the demand for bank deposits, which is a cost to the firms. The second term is negative: the same increase, by making securities more profitable, reduces the demand for deposits. For the firms to draw an advantage from increasing the yield offered on securities, the net result should be negative. This result would be more probable the more savers react to a change in the yield on securities when deciding the composition of their financial portfolios.

## 6.3   Interest paid on bank loans

Let us now consider interest paid by firms on loans granted to them by banks. It is evident that interest can be actually paid by the firms (and not simply by merely acknowledging the debt) only if the firms command the required liquidity coming from a source not connected to a bank loan. In fact, if the only liquidity in existence originates from bank loans, the firms, by selling commodities and issuing securities, will at best get back the money they have initially spent. This means that firms will be able at best to repay the principal but not the interest on the loans granted them by the banks.

Let us now consider the problem from the viewpoint of the banks. The interest payments that the banks receive from firms are partly used to cover current costs (such as wages and salaries to employees), and partly are net profits to be used for purchasing real goods (such as investment in real estate or other forms of real goods). If net profits of the banks are used to make purchases in the commodities market, the two payments cancel out.

In technical terms, the situation might be depicted as follows. The banks advance to the firms the liquidity required for the payment of interest and spend at the same time an equal amount of liquidity on goods and services. The receipts from such sales are used by firms to repay their bank debt. The final result is that firms pay their interest debt in kind. In fact, since in our simplified case no other money exists beyond that created by means of bank credit, the firms have only two ways of paying interest to the banks, namely acknowledging the debt while letting it increase without limit over time, or paying it in kind.[1]

If firms as a whole pay their interest debt in kind, thereby giving up a part of their product to the banks, this means that the aggregate product remaining after paying real wages (the classical authors would call it 'net product', others 'surplus product') is divided between banks and firms, or, as some might prefer to say, between industrial and financial capital.

---

[1] Lavoie 1987; Graziani 1984. As already recalled, a similar solution is rejected by Wray (1996: 452) and accepted by Bossone (2001: 869, 873).

The share of aggregate product that the firms pass on to the banks clearly depends (a) on the level of the interest rate set by the banks when granting loans to the firms and (b) on the level of prices set by the firms when selling commodities to the banks. A high level of interest rates could therefore induce firms to protect their own profits by setting a higher level of prices. High interest rates might therefore be a source of inflation.

## 6.4   A model with bank credit

Let us assume the following notation:

$Z=$ total monetary base
$Z_B =$ legal tender held by the banks
$Z_P =$ legal tender held by the public
$D=$ deposits
$r=$ reserve ratio of commercial banks
$w=$ money wage rate
$c, s=$ propensities to consume and to save
$N=$ employment
$i_D =$ interest rate on bank deposits
$i_L =$ interest rate on bank loans
$i_B =$ interest rate on securities.

### The initial situation

Let us assume legal tender and deposits to be demanded in a constant ratio $\beta$:

$Z_P = \beta D.$

Since, owing to the compulsory reserve ratio $r$, $Z_B = rD$, the total monetary base will be:

$$Z = Z_B + Z_P + (r + \beta)D = \left(1 + \frac{\beta}{r}\right) Z_B. \qquad (6.1)$$

The liquid balances of the public (legal tender plus deposits) are:

$$Z_P + D = (1 + \text{\ss})D = \frac{1 + \text{\ss}}{r} Z_B. \tag{6.2}$$

If we consider producers as a single integrated and consolidated sector, the loans granted by the banks $L_{(1)}$ at the beginning of the period equal the current wage bill plus the pre-existing money stock $M^0$ (the amount $M^0$ equals households' liquid balances coming from previous periods and at the same time the residual debt of producers at the beginning of the new period):

$$L_{(1)} = M^0 + wN_{(1)}, \tag{6.3}$$

where the subscript (1) indicates the situation at the beginning of the period. Therefore we can write:

$$Z_{P(1)} + D_{(1)} = \frac{1 + \text{\ss}}{r} Z_{B(1)} = M^0 + wN_{(1)} \tag{6.2'}$$

and:

$$Z_{B(1)} = \frac{r}{1 + \text{\ss}}(M^0 + wN_{(1)}).$$

This value for $Z_{B(1)}$ can be substituted into (6.1):

$$Z_{(1)} = \left(1 + \frac{\text{\ss}}{r}\right) \frac{r}{1 + \text{\ss}}(M^0 + wN_{(1)}) = \frac{r + \text{\ss}}{1 + \text{\ss}}(M^0 + wN_{(1)}). \tag{6.1'}$$

The stock of money in existence immediately after the wage bill has been paid and before households take their expenditure and savings decisions depends strictly on the wage bill, and therefore on the level of output, decided by producers.

### The equilibrium conditions

In the model of a monetary economy such as the one we are now considering, the definition of equilibrium diverges considerably from the usual one. In the theory of general economic equilibrium, each single agent is required to observe his own budget constraint, which means that, in equilibrium, no single agent can have debts pending towards any other agent. The only exception is the government sector, since it is generally admitted that in equilibrium government expenditure can be covered by debt, be it interest-bearing debt (government bonds in the hands of private agents) or non-interest-bearing debt (liquid balances advanced by the central bank). In fact it is also debatable whether the presence of a certain amount of government debt implies a real divergence from general equilibrium. As previously recalled (§2.2). it is commonly admitted that in a monetary economy agents may hold money as protection against contingencies: an amount of government debt towards the central bank allows the government, by means of deficit spending, to satisfy such needs of private agents. The result is that the budget deficit run by the government performs the function of supplying a useful commodity (liquid balances) to the private sector. To the extent to which the government, when spending newly created liquidity, is in fact selling a commodity required by the market, the substance of a deficit disappears.

In a simplified model considering only the private sector, the situation is different. Also here the presence of money holdings in the hands of private agents should be considered as normal. But the money in existence is no longer a debt of the government to the central bank but a debt of the firms to the banks. So long as money holdings are considered a normal element of a monetary economy, an equilibrium position need not imply the full payment of all debts but allows instead the presence of a debt owed by firms to the banks.

On the other hand the precise amount of firms' debt consistent with an equilibrium position cannot be defined. Even in the simple case of a stationary economy it would be erroneous to define constancy of firms' debt as a necessary requirement of equilibrium. In fact any increase in the liquidity preference of single agents requires, even in stationary conditions, an equal change in the equilibrium money stock and therefore an increase in the firms' debt towards the banks. A similar increase has no implications either for the efficiency of firms or for the soundness of their financial position, nor does it imply a divergence from general equilibrium (this point was also recognised by Hayek 1978).

The problem of defining an equilibrium therefore reduces to an analysis of the banks' attitude towards the debt of the firms. A first case to be examined is the case of an increase in the liquidity propensity of agents in a stationary economy. When this happens, once agents have brought their money holdings to the desired level, they resume distributing their income between commodities and securities without making any further addition to their liquid balances. The bank debt of the firms is now once more stable, even if higher than before. If the banks accept the new level of the firms' debt, the economy is again in equilibrium.

A second possibility is that operators decide instead regularly to increase the share of their current income to be held as money. In this case the banks are confronted with a continuously increasing debt owed by firms. If the banks refuse to continuously increase the loans granted to firms, firms will be forced to reduce their activity level. At the same time, a parallel negative reaction might come from firms in terms of a reduction in investment plans, since an increasing bank debt, even if not depending on any inefficiency of the firms and being only a consequence of an increased liquidity preference of the public, negatively affects the firms' profits.

If the banking system is reluctant to grant higher loans, or if the firms themselves are reluctant to let their bank debt increase, firms might try to balance the increase in savers' liquidity preference by offering higher interest rates on the securities they issue. As we know, an increase in interest rates paid on securities does not affect the firms' profits and therefore should not induce them to revise their investment plans. However it cannot be ruled out that, when interest on securities is increased, the banks will also increase the rates charged on their loans. If this happens, even if by way of an indirect mechanism, any increase in the liquidity preference of the public may bring about a fall in investment and activity levels.

## The final situation

The relationships between banks and firms give rise to three kinds of interest rates: (a) a rate on banks loans, paid by the firms to the banks; (b) a rate on bank deposits, possibly reckoned by the banks to their depositors; and (c) a rate on securities paid by firms to savers.

Firms, as already said, make use of the interest rate on securities in order to make more attractive the securities they issue, thus reducing their bank debt. Banks can similarly use the rate they pay on deposits in order to make deposits more attractive to savers, thereby forcing firms to increase their bank debt and increasing the volume of the loans they grant. On this ground, competition takes place between banks and firms.

Household savings are distributed between an increase in liquid holdings ($dM^d$) and an increase in holdings of securities issued by producers ($dB^d$). The purchase of new securities is a fraction $b^d$ of total savings:

$$S = (1 - c)wN = dM^d + dB^d$$
$$dM^d = (1 - b^d)(1 - c)wN.$$

The fraction $b^b$ of total savings placed in securities can be assumed to be an increasing function of the interest rate paid on securities ($i_B$) and a decreasing function of the interest rate reckoned by banks on deposits ($i_D$):

$$b^d = b^d(i_B/i_D).$$

The demand for securities at the end of the period, inclusive of the amount $B^0$ of securities outstanding at the beginning of the same period, can therefore be defined as:

$$B^d_{(2)} = B^0 + b^d(i_B/i_D)(1 - c)wN \tag{6.4}$$

(the subscript (2) indicates the situation at the end of the period).

The supply of securities on the part of producers aims at collecting in the financial market the total amount of household savings. If the target is reached, producers are able to repay at least the principal of their initial bank debt (the problem of how to repay interest has been dealt with in §3). The possibility, as well as the convenience, of fully attaining the target depends on the prevailing level and structure of interest rates. If rates in the financial market are very high while banks are ready to grant loans at reasonable rates, it can turn out to be more convenient to producers to drop the idea of collecting the whole of current savings and keep a portion of their bank debt pending.

This means that the supply of securities on the part of producers will equal a fraction $b^s$ of total savings, $b^s$ being a decreasing function of the interest rate on securities ($i_B$) and an increasing function of the interest rate on bank loans ($i_L$):

$$B^S_{(2)} = B^0 + b^S(i_L/i_B)(1 - c)wN.$$

The equilibrium condition in the financial market can be written as:

$$b^d(i_B/i_D) = b^s(i_L/i_B) = b, \tag{6.5}$$

where $b$ is the equilibrium value of the fraction of savings placed in securities.

Since there are three unknowns ($i_D, i_L, i_B$), the equilibrium condition can determine only one of the three as a function of the other two. If, for instance, the interest rate on deposits is given (in many cases it might be assumed to be close to zero), the equilibrium condition determines the ratio $i_L/i_B$

that must prevail between the interest rate on loans made by banks and the interest rate on securities issued by producers.

The bank debt of producers outstanding at the end of the period will be equal to the debt at the beginning of the period minus the amount of new securities issued by producers and sold to savers:

$$L_{(2)} = M^0 + wN - b(1-c)wN$$
$$= M^0 + [1 - b(1-c)]wN.$$

As previously mentioned, this condition does not mean that producers will be able wholly to repay their bank debt. Of course we can also make the specific assumption that producers only consider themselves in equilibrium if the new bank debt (or at least the principal of the new bank debt) incurred at the beginning of the period has been repaid at the end (which means that their bank debt is stable). With a stable bank debt, the money stock is also constant. This reminds us of the Keynesian assumption of the *General Theory*, according to which the money supply is assumed to be constant and, as already remarked, suggests the idea that, in assuming a given money stock, Keynes might have had in mind not just a mere simplification but an equilibrium condition of producers vis-à-vis the banks.

In this case the equilibrium condition should be written as:

$$b^d(i_B/i_D) = b^S(i_L/i_B) = 1. \tag{6.5'}$$

Having assumed $i_D$ to be given, the resulting value of $i_L/i_B$ determines the ratio between the interest rate on loans charged by the banks and the interest rate on securities issued by producers that should prevail for the stock of money to be constant. It will be noticed that, as in the Keynesian model, the rate of interest (in this case the ratio between the two rates present in the model) is totally independent of the savings ratio and depends on the relative preference of the agents between liquidity and securities as well as on the criteria followed by producers in managing their debt (a higher bank debt versus an issue of new securities).

Equilibrium in the financial market can be given a graphical representation. Let us assume the following values for $b^d$ and $b^s$:

$$b^d = \frac{i_B}{\beta^2 i_D^2}; \quad b^s = \frac{i_L^2}{\mu^2 i_B},$$

where ß is a measure of the liquidity preference of savers. If the interest rate on securities is such that $i_B = \beta^2 i_D^2$, $b^d$ equals unity and current savings are entirely spent in the financial market. The parameter $\mu$ reflects the preference of producers for bank credit with respect to issuing securities. If by any chance the interest rate on bank loans is such that: $i_L^2 = \mu^2 i_B$, $b^s$ equals unity and producers issue securities in an amount equivalent to savings.

The equilibrium condition, $b^d = b^s$, gives as a solution:

$$i_B = \frac{\beta}{\mu} i_L i_D$$

and:

$$b = \frac{i_B}{\beta^2 i_D^2}.$$

It was made clear beforehand that it would be wrong to suppose that a stationary equilibrium necessarily requires that the quantity of money is constant. On the other hand, it is quite possible that firms consider their own financial situation to be in equilibrium when, money revenues and outlays being equal, their bank debt is constant. If this is the case, when the equilibrium condition required by the firms obtains, the money stock will also be constant.[2] A similar condition deserves closer analysis.

[2] As already noted above, it is a common, even if not unanimous, interpretation of the *General Theory* that Keynes assumes the money stock to be given and constant. The rationale for a similar assumption might be not of making the model simpler, nor of assuming that the only source of money

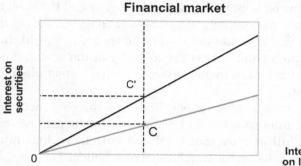

Figure 6.1   Real and financial equilibrium

In the special case in which: $b^d = b^s = 1$, and the money stock is constant, the equilibrium condition, $b^d = b^s$, gives as a solution:

$$\frac{i_B}{\beta^2 i_D^2} = \frac{i_L^2}{\mu^2 i_B}$$

and:

$$i_B = \frac{\beta}{\mu} i_D i_L.$$

A representation of this condition is given in figure 6.1. The diagram shows the possible equilibrium positions from a Keynesian viewpoint. Each of the increasing lines is the locus of all points corresponding to a constant money stock, and therefore to a financial equilibrium of the firms. The two lines appearing in the figure correspond to two different values of ß (for a higher ß the curve is correspondingly higher: a higher ß corresponds to a higher liquidity preference). Point $C$ is a hypothetical equilibrium in which the interest rate on securities gives rise to a volume of investment corresponding to a full employment income. A higher value of ß shifts the equilibrium line upwards. If $i_L$ is unchanged, the economy

be the government deficit, but of introducing a condition defining firms' financial equilibrium.

will now be in point $C'$, $i_B$ will be higher and the level of activity correspondingly lower. Since at point $C'$ the condition $b = 1$ is satisfied as before, producers are in equilibrium so far as their bank debt is concerned. But the economy is out of equilibrium in that a certain amount of unemployment is present.

The condition for full equilibrium is therefore twofold: the rate of interest must be low enough for investment to rise to the full employment level and current savings must be fully invested in the purchase of new bonds. The result has a specific weight in that it points out that for full equilibrium to be attained, two different conditions have to be satisfied. The first is the usual Keynesian condition that the interest rate and the corresponding level of investment be such as to generate a full-employment level of activity. The second is that a financial equilibrium between banks and firms prevails. The second condition is often neglected in macroeconomic analysis since, as already remarked, in most macroeconomic models, banks and firms are merged into one single sector.

Once more, the stock of money in existence at the end of the period appears to be a strictly endogenous variable. This result is a direct consequence of the fact that the amount of money created at the beginning of the period and not destroyed at the end equals the increase in money balances required by agents at the end of the period, a magnitude that the monetary authorities can modify only indirectly by manipulating the structure of the interest rates. Neither can the amount be reduced by the banks: all the banks can do is to reduce the amount of new credit granted to firms, but they cannot cancel old loans not yet repaid.

At the end of the period, the liquid balances are reduced, as compared to their amount at the beginning of the period, by an amount equal to the amount of expenditure by households in the goods market plus the amount of securities bought by savers. The same applies to bank deposits and to the monetary base.

# 7

# Real and monetary interest

## 7.1 The theory of the real interest rate

The transition from a traditional model, where, in equilibrium, the only stock of money existing is money created by the government sector, to an enlarged model allowing for the existence, also in equilibrium, of credit money supplied by the banks, produces at least one remarkable consequence concerning the doctrine of real and monetary interest rates.[1]

The received doctrine can be synthetically set forth as follows. Anyone granting a money loan runs the risk of seeing the purchasing power of money eroded by inflation in the interval between the time the loan is granted and the time the loan is repaid. If this happens, the loaner gets back a sum having a lower real value than the sum initially lent, and so suffers a capital loss. In order to avoid a loss, the loan should be adequately indexed in order to eliminate the influence of any possible increase in the level of money prices.

Two possible kinds of indexation are conceivable: real and financial.

---

[1] The distinction between the real and the monetary rates of interest, already outlined by Henry Thornton (1939 [1811]: 335–6), and John Stuart Mill (1909 [1848], book III, chapter 23, §4: 645–6), was first presented in a complete form by Alfred Marshall (1961 [1920], book VI, chapter 6, §7: 593–5) and finally codified by Irving Fisher (1896: 13–14). An account of the long controversy is contained in Graziani 1983.

*Real indexation* (or ex-post indexation, or indexation on capital) is an agreement that the basis for the annual interest payments is *r*, the rate that would prevail with no inflation, and that an extra repayment linked to inflation will be made at the end of the loan, when the principal is revalued according to such inflation as may have occurred. In this case, the extra payment made by the debtor on account of the increase in prices is concentrated at the end of the loan, and the inflation rate considered no longer reflects expected inflation but actual inflation.

*Financial indexation* (or ex-ante indexation, or indexation on interest) is an agreement that the principal will be repaid at its nominal value, while the current interest rate is increased in order to allow for expected inflation. In this case, current interest payments are higher while the principal will be repaid in nominal terms, which means that in real terms it will be correspondingly reduced. The substance is that the debtor, when paying the yearly interest, is also repaying a portion of the principal.

If the indexation is correct, the two forms should be equivalent and the two alternative flows of payments made by the debtor, while different in their time shapes, should be equal in their present values. Of the two, financial indexation is the form more frequently produced by the spontaneous working of the market.

Irving Fisher introduced a formula for financial indexation which is still adopted for defining the real rate of interest. Let us denote by *r* the rate that would prevail in case of no inflation (a rate that may be called *real rate of interest*), *i* as the rate actually agreed upon (the *money rate of interest*), and $\varphi$ as the expected inflation rate. For the consequences of inflation to be neutralised, the sum to be paid back, $M_t$, should equal the sum initially lent $M_0$ revalued according to the expected inflation rate $\varphi$:

$$M_t = M_0(1 + \varphi).$$

If we add the interest rate $r$, the total repayment will be:

$$M_t = M_0(1 + \varphi)(1 + r) = M_0(1 + r + \varphi + r\varphi).$$

This is the complete Fisher formula: $r$ is the real interest rate, $\varphi$ is added as an indexation of the principal; $r\varphi$ represents an indexation of the interest payments. Since this last term is presumably very small, it can be neglected, thus reducing the formula to:

$$M_t = M_0(1 + r + \varphi).$$

This was the formula initially suggested by Marshall in simple non-algebraic terms. We can conclude that, if the expected inflation rate is $\varphi$, the monetary rate of interest will be:

$$i = r + \varphi.$$

As Fisher himself emphasised, indexation, whatever its form, can only be applied if the possibility of future inflation is actually taken into account by the contracting agents. Sudden unexpected inflation waves prevent any possible kind of indexation, ex ante or ex post, real or financial, and produce a serious redistribution of wealth, hitting creditors and favouring debtors.[2]

## 7.2 The real interest rate and endogenous money

The doctrine of the real interest rate as formulated by Marshall and Fisher is formally unobjectionable. However, the

---

[2] It is a well-known fact that Keynes did not agree with Fisher on the fact that, when inflation is foreseen, indexation will be put into practice. In Keynes's view, no such thing as a commonly expected inflation can occur. The moment an increase in prices comes to be expected by all agents in the market, prices will go up immediately. The sudden increase in prices will hit all those who are in possession of liquid assets as well as creditors and it will be too late for them to take measures affording protection against it (Keynes 1973a [1936], book IV, chapter 2, §3: 142).

same doctrine is strictly connected to the neoclassical approach to monetary theory. As already remarked (§2.4), in the neoclassical approach, the whole of the money stock existing in equilibrium is considered to originate from government deficit and any inflationary phenomenon is brought back to an excess demand from the government sector. Government expenditure is viewed both as a source of inflation and as the origin of the liquidity necessary to sustain it.

The perspective is modified if we look at the problem from a different viewpoint; that is if we consider excess demand as coming from the non-government sector and the necessary increase in the money stock as originating in an increasing amount of bank loans. Let us consider the simplest model of the circulation approach, a model in which liquidity is only created by the banking sector and no money is produced by government deficit. Money is introduced into the market by producers who go into debt to the banks in order to pay their wage bill. The money existing in the market and allowing exchanges to take place is equal to the loans granted by the banks to producers. This means that an inflationary process requires a continuous increase in the bank debt of producers.

Let us now examine the financial position of producers. Consider a hypothetical case of a regular, fully foreseen, inflation, proceeding at a constant rate and taking place in a stationary economy in which producers employ a constant number of workers and produce a constant level of output. Inflation in itself forces producers to increase their bank debt, thereby increasing their nominal financial burden. To be precise, the consequence of inflation is that, even if the interest rate is constant, the nominal financial burden falling on producers grows at a constant rate equal to the inflation rate. If, in addition to that, the rate of interest is increased according to the Fisher formula, the financial burden of firms grows over time at a rate that is twice the inflation rate. This is due to the fact that producers are forced to expand their bank debt and, in addition to that, the interest rate paid on each monetary unit borrowed from the banks is increased, according to Fisher's principle, by an amount equal to the rate of inflation.

In order to measure in real terms the financial burden falling on producers, the monetary measure of the burden must be deflated in proportion to the inflation rate. The result is that, if the Fisher formula is applied, inflation increases the financial burden in real terms by a rate equal to the inflation rate. Linking the nominal interest rate to a price index, a measure conceived for ensuring a constant real value of the debt, produces the opposite consequence: the real burden of the debt is increased, with a consequent redistribution of wealth against producers (the debtors) and in favour of the banks (the creditors).

## 7.3 A formal presentation

The case can be outlined in more rigorous terms as follows. Let us consider a stationary economy in which employment is constant and equal to $N$, the productivity of labour is also constant and equal to $\pi$, and total output is $X$. Let us imagine, to begin with, an equilibrium position with stable prices and wages ($p_0$, $w_0$). In a fully competitive equilibrium, profits are eliminated and the value of output equals total costs, the remuneration of producers being included in the cost of production.

Total costs incurred by producers are equal to the wage bill plus interest due to the banks. The equilibrium condition of firms is therefore:

$$\pi N p_0 = w_0 N (1 + r), \tag{7.1}$$

where the first term denotes the producers' receipts (the value of output) and the second term denotes the producers' costs (the wage bill plus interest to be paid to the banks).

*Case 1*: Let us examine first a case of inflation financed by government deficit, a case typical of the neoclassical approach to monetary theory. We may call this a case of *external inflation*. At the beginning of each period, firms take out bank loans equal in amount to the wage bill, measured according to the initial level of the wage rate $w_0$ (above, §1.8). Let us imagine that an inflation rate equal to $\varphi$ is expected. The banks, following the Fisher rule, will set a money rate of interest equal to:

$$i = (1 + r)(1 + \varphi).$$

At the end of the period, the bank debt of producers will be:

$$D = w_0 N(1 + r)(1 + \varphi).$$

If the expectations are fulfilled, inflation exactly equal to $\varphi$ takes place. This means that producers, without going into more debt, sell their output at prices that are now equal to $p_0(1 + \varphi)$. The receipts of producers are now:

$$R = \pi N p_0(1 + \varphi).$$

It is easy to see that, if producers were in equilibrium at the initial price level (that is if the producers' receipts were equal to their bank debt), the same equilibrium will prevail now:

$$\pi N p_0(1 + \varphi) = w_0 N(1 + r)(1 + \varphi) \tag{7.2}$$

(in fact, if (7.1) holds, (7.2) must also hold). In this case, the Fisher rule applies and indexation of the interest rate leaves the real positions of debtors and creditors unchanged.

*Case 2*: Let us now come to the case of an inflation financed by bank credit, an inflation that can be called *internal inflation*. In this case, as already said, the money stock is increased by the action of the banks and by their granting higher and higher loans to producers. In each period producers, in order to face the increasing level of wages and prices that they themselves co-operate to produce, need a higher amount of initial finance, their bank debt increasing at the same rate as inflation. If the expected inflation rate is $\varphi$, producers will need, in each period $t$, bank loans $F_t$ equal to:

$$F_t = w_0 N(1 + \varphi)^t.$$

Let us imagine, to begin with, that, in spite of expected inflation, the interest rate remains at a level $r$ that would prevail in a situation of stable prices. The monetary receipts of producers in the first period of inflation will be:

$$\pi N p_1 = \pi N p_0 (1 + \varphi).$$

It is easy to see that, if producers were in equilibrium at the initial prices, that is if in each period their receipts were equal to their bank debt, the same will be true at the new higher level of prices:

$$\pi N p_0 (1 + \varphi) = w_0 N(1 + r)(1 + \varphi) \tag{7.3}$$

since, once more, if (7.1) holds, (7.3) will also hold.

The situation will be different if the interest rate is adjusted to inflation according to the Fisher rule. In that case, the money value of the sales is the one just indicated, but the bank debt of producers, measured at the new interest rate $i = r + \varphi + \varphi r$, is now equal to:

$$D = w_0 N(1 + r)(1 + \varphi)^2.$$

Even if producers' receipts and costs were balanced before inflation, they will be unbalanced now, since:

$$\pi N p_0 (1 + \varphi) < w_0 N(1 + r)(1 + \varphi)^2.$$

A first conclusion emerges: Fisher's doctrine of the real interest rate cannot be considered a general principle always valid. It is a correct principle only in the case in which money, being created by government deficit, *is not a debt of producers towards the banks.*

The above conclusion is, however, not a final one. In fact, the same considerations developed above in connection to the private sector must apply to the government sector.[3]

When analysing the case of producers, we made a distinction between two possible cases of inflation, the first one being the case of an inflation financed by the government's deficit, the second of an inflation financed by bank credit. The crucial difference between the two cases lies in the fact that, in the first, the rate of increase in the bank debt of firms equals the rate of increase in prices, while in the second (if the Fisher formula is applied), firms' debt increases at a rate twice as high as the rate of inflation.

The reverse is true if we consider the consequences of inflation on government debt. In an inflationary situation, the government is forced to increase its nominal budget deficit, if only in order to keep expenditure constant in real terms. If inflation is financed by government deficit, the government is hit twice: its debt to the central bank increases and the rate of interest paid on government bonds also increases. If inflation is financed by bank credit granted to private firms, the increase in government expenditure is financed by an increase in tax receipts and the government is hit only once, namely by the increase in the rate of interest.

Historical experience shows that money is created both by government deficit and by bank credit. If, as usually happens, inflation produces an adjustment of interest rates according to the Fisher rule, both the government and producers are damaged in proportion to the quantity of money that each has helped to create by going into debt respectively with the central bank and with commercial banks. A corresponding

[3] The specific problem of the correct measurement of the real burden of the debt falling on the government has been raised and analysed in detail by Modigliani and Cohn (1979). Their analysis is, however, only partially valid since they neglect the fact that, in inflation, the government (as well as producers) not only has to pay a higher rate of interest but is also forced to increase its current nominal expenditure if expenditure is to remain constant in real terms.

advantage for the banks emerges: in fact, the total nominal receipts of the banks are increased for the dual reason that interest rates are revised upwards and that the amount of loans is increased, while in order to measure receipts in real terms, the same receipts have to be deflated just once.

The traditional doctrine of the real interest rate therefore has a limited validity, in that it only applies to the private sector and only in the case in which the whole of the money supply is created by government deficit.

# 8

---

# Implications for monetary policy

## 8.1  A basic issue: the endogenous nature of money

In discussing the implications of the circuit approach for monetary policy, a first preliminary issue has to be made clear concerning the nature and meaning of the assumption of endogenous money. In most macroeconomic models the money stock is treated as a given variable. A question remains open. When a variable is considered as a parameter, three possible interpretations are present:

a)  The variable may be in the nature of a technical constant; a case which can be immediately set aside when the variable in question is the stock of money.

b)  The variable may be considered as a parameter. In this case, its exact value is left undetermined and the analysis is meant to apply whatever the value of the parameter may be (this might be the meaning implied in Keynes's *General Theory*, when the author considers the money stock as given).

c)  The variable may be determined by forces lying outside the model, for instance, in the case of the money stock, by the monetary authorities. This is perhaps the meaning implied in most macroeconomic models when dealing with the quantity of money. Of course, if a rule of conduct for the monetary authorities is defined and inserted as an integral part of the model, the money stock is no longer an exogenous variable and is endogenously determined by the solution of the model.

When introducing the concept of endogenous money, similar doubts can arise. In general, an endogenous money stock is defined as a variable determined inside the model. A description of the process of creation, circulation and destruction of money should therefore be provided and the model should include equations defining the demand and supply of the different kinds of money (be it legal tender, bank deposits, or whatever is used in the market for the exchange of goods).[1] It should, however, be emphasised that a more restricted, and extremely simplified, meaning is often implied, in that by endogenous money the case is meant in which the money stock is simply taken as equal to the demand for money balances. This is the case with authors who, like Kaldor and his followers, consider the banking system and the monetary authorities as forcefully held to satisfy any demand for money coming from the market.

When considering the problem of steering the economy by controlling the stock of money, it is clear that in the last case (money stock entirely determined by demand) any possibility of using the quantity of money as a policy instrument is ruled out. In this extreme case, the definition of the money stock as an endogenous variable carries in itself the idea that monetary policy is an instrument of limited validity.

## 8.2   The problem of monetary stability

A common prescription connects the level of money prices to the quantity of money introduced by way of a government deficit. It is also commonly accepted that the increase in money prices is influenced by the way a government deficit is financed: more precisely, it will be higher if the government

---

[1] An example of a similar analysis is to be found in Messori 1988.

deficit is financed by printing money, lower if financed by issuing securities.

The analysis performed in the preceding chapters shows that money prices do not depend, except indirectly, on the quantity of money and that therefore they also do not depend directly on how a government deficit is financed. The technique of financing a deficit does have an effect on prices, but only in an indirect way, and the effect produced is opposite to what the dominant analysis indicates. In fact a deficit financed by issuing government bonds increases the amount of interest payments and therefore the money incomes of savers; the consequence is that money prices are pushed upwards more than if the same deficit were financed by money creation. In terms of our equations of §5.4, a similar result is produced by an increase in the amount of bonds in existence $B$. In a context of endogenous money, an increase in income will also produce an increase in the money stock. But, as Keynes would say, while the level of prices and the stock of money increase together, the direction of change is reversed, in that the increase in the quantity of money is a consequence and not a prerequisite of the increase in prices (Keynes 1971 [1930], chapter 11: 156–9; *Collected Writings*, vol. 6: 141–3).

It need not be added that the technique of financing a government deficit exerts a direct influence on the level of interest rates. In fact, if government expenditure is increased without increasing the stock of money, an increase in the rate of interest will be inevitable in order to finance the increased amount of transactions connected to a higher level of income with a constant quantity of money.

## 8.3   Inflation and profits

It is a well-known fact that expected inflation brings an increase in interest rates. The increase in the rate of interest on loans is in fact required by creditors in order to protect their loan from the erosion produced by inflation. A common belief is that if actual inflation equals expected inflation, the indexation of interest is fair: the time shape of repayments, if measured in real terms, will be changed but the total value of the debt will be unaltered. The preceding analysis shows that a similar conclusion may be valid only in the case in which the existing money stock has been totally created by the government deficit. In a framework of endogenous money, such as the one adopted in the circuit approach, where money is a private debt of the firms towards the banks, the opposite conclusion prevails. Inflation, if defined as a continuous increase in money prices, brings about in itself a proportional increase in the bank debt of the firms. If an increase in the rate of interest proportional to the inflation rate is added to the increase in the amount of the debt, the annual financial burden falling on firms is increased in money terms by an amount equal to twice the inflation rate. In real terms, the financial burden of the firms is increased in proportion to the inflation rate.

A similar conclusion has considerable relevance in terms of economic policy. Inflation can damage firms on the labour market, if workers ask for a precautionary increase in wages even before an increase in the cost of living. But, beyond the labour market, firms can lose profits on a second frontier: the credit market. In a context of an endogenous money supply, inflation produces a redistribution of profits from the firms to the banks, which implies a decline in industrial profits and an increase in financial profits. While the firms can compensate for losses in the labour market by increasing money prices, they are unable to compensate for losses in the credit market when interest rates rise. In fact any increase in prices forces them to make recourse to additional borrowing, with a consequent increase in the financial burden falling on them.

Since industrial profits are considered a privileged source of finance for investment, there may be a common interest in protecting profits in order to stimulate economic growth.

Protection of profits can be obtained by acting on two sides – by a policy of wage containment and by a policy of low interest rates. Low interest rates on the credit market can be obtained by reducing the official discount rate; low rates on the financial market can be obtained by inducing firms to offer more liquid and easily marketable securities, thus making them more attractive to savers who tend to avoid illiquid placements.

The choice between the two possible lines of action has clear political implications. It depends on the social views of policy makers and on external constraints such as the trend of interest rates on the international capital market. It is, however, an important contribution of the circuit approach to point out the fact that in an inflationary situation, when financial indexation according to the Fisher rule is applied, industrial profits, even absent any pressure coming from the labour market, tend to be reduced by the operation of the credit market.

The same conclusion applies to financial markets, and in particular to the case of government debt. In inflation, the money yield of government securities is likely to increase along with the general level of interest rates. In general, it can also be assumed, even though no precise rule can be given, that government expenditure tends to be set in real terms. This means that inflation exerts two consequences on the financial burden falling on the government. In the first place, indexation of the interest rate, if applied according to the Fisher rule, anticipates in part the repayment of the principal. So far, inflation alters the time shape of payments without modifying the total weight of the financial burden. At most, since the increase in the yearly real burden of debt, due to the increased yearly interest payments, is apparent while the decrease in the real value of the final repayment goes unnoticed, the illusion may arise of a higher total burden. But, as shown beforehand, in contrast to the prevailing opinion, a second consequence is also present in that, just as for private debt, inflation coupled to the Fisher rule increases the real burden of government debt.

The policy lesson to be drawn is that in periods of inflation any government deficit should be covered by increasing the money stock (a debt towards the central bank requiring a nominal interest payment) rather than by making recourse to the financial market and to savers.

## 8.4   The distribution of real income

An even more relevant policy consequence concerns the distribution of real income. The circuit approach shows that the distribution of real income between wages and profits is strictly connected to the independent decisions of producers and to the subdivision of production between consumption goods and capital goods. Such decisions, taken at the real level, bypass any distribution or redistribution of money income performed by altering the payments made to factors of production. The same decisions also overcome any redistribution performed by taxation. In fact, it has been shown that even in the extreme case in which taxes are levied only on profits and subsidies paid entirely to wage earners, the distribution of real income is not affected.

The policy lesson to be drawn is clear. If the government wants to alter the distribution of real income against profits and in favour of wages, it is no use working by means of monetary taxes and subsidies. The government should instead provide goods and services in real terms and make them available to those social groups whose real income it seems desirable to increase.

# 9

---

# Concluding remarks

## 9.1  General features of the circulation approach

In its more general aspect, the so-called circulation approach to the analysis of the economic process is no more than a presentation of the successive phases describing the creation, circulation and final destruction of money. While in itself this should not give rise to fundamental divergences from the more traditional and still dominant theory, it so happens that in a number of specific, but vital, cases the conclusions reached by the circulation approach seem to be radically different. The main divergences can be synthesised as follows.

## 9.2  The nature of the market

In the neoclassical model, the market, so long as perfect competition prevails, is considered as a totally democratic and egalitarian mechanism. Any inequalities in the distribution of income and wealth do not depend on the operation of the market mechanism itself, since agents are admitted to negotiations on an equal footing, no matter what the nature or the amount of the goods and services demanded or supplied may be. Of course agents endowed with a higher purchasing power will exert a greater influence on the equilibrium price as compared to less-endowed agents; but, while this may be considered as a case of unequal power, it depends on an unequal income distribution and not on the working of the market per se.

If, always remaining within the neoclassical perspective, we enquire about the possible origins of the inequalities in income distribution, these will appear as being largely justified. Inequalities in income from labour should be ascribed to different innate abilities of single agents, or to differences in the professional formations and therefore to different investments made in human capital before entering the labour market. Inequalities in income from capital, originating from an unequal distribution in property and wealth, should be ascribed to different saving propensities either of the agents themselves or of preceding generations who have transmitted to their heirs the fortunes in their possession. The conclusion is that the income of which any agent can dispose wholly originates from labour or from saving of the agent himself or of his predecessors. The fact that single agents may enjoy a fortune accumulated thanks to the thrift of others may seem unfair. But, it should be recognised that accumulating wealth not only for oneself but also for one's descendants is a natural tendency of any individual; in addition to that, as the received doctrine points out, if wealth left to one's descendants were severely taxed, the propensity to save of single agents might be greatly reduced, with possible detrimental effects for the whole community in the long run.

According to the circulation approach, the mechanism of the market appears in a wholly different light. In a monetary economy, the fact of being endowed with real productive resources, no matter whether real goods or labour skills, doesn't imply in itself the possibility of entering the market and buying a fraction of the available product or of being endowed with any purchasing power. This is especially true of wage earners: if unemployed, they have no access to the market, whatever their abilities may be; if employed they get a monetary income the level of which in real terms escapes any possible previous determination or negotiation.

In a monetary economy, access to the market no longer depends on having real resources available but on having the required amount of means of payment. As seen above, in a monetary economy only firms, thanks to their having access to credit and to the consequent availability of liquid means, determine the level of activity, the real consumption of wage earners and the rate of capital accumulation, and only they can acquire the property of new means of production. The purchasing power pertaining to wage earners depends on autonomous decisions taken by producers.

## 9.3　Real income and wealth

The different treatment enjoyed by different groups on the market affects the nature of the wealth owned by each of them.

The circulation approach emphasises the fact that financial wealth, held by savers in the form of securities or bank deposits, is not real wealth for owners as a whole. No doubt, if individual savers succeed in selling part or all of their financial wealth to others, they will be able to increase their own real consumption; single agents, therefore, by making use of financial wealth set aside, are able to modify the time shape of their own real consumption. But the same is not true of savers as a whole. In fact if all savers should decide to sell part of their wealth in order to increase their current consumption, they would be unable to find buyers (and even if they could, their expenditure on the commodities market would only increase prices without any actual increase in real consumption).

If financial wealth is not real wealth of wage earners as a group, this means that to them the level of real income equals the level of real consumption. Moreover, as the circulation approach shows, the level of real consumption of wage earners as a whole is determined by the amount of consumer goods that firms decide to produce. In the monetary theory of production there is no place for any autonomous role of consumers; the principle of consumer sovereignty is wholly ignored and replaced by the opposite principle of the sovereignty of producers. The same is also true in the presence of government expenditure. Investments decided by firms, being totally autonomous, cannot be crowded out by government expenditure; they rather crowd out household consumption.

Having eliminated consumer sovereignty and replaced it by a principle of sovereignty of producers, the theory defines the market equilibrium differently and gives it a different meaning. Indeed, in the monetary theory of production equilibrium need not be unique or stable. The theory allows for a multiplicity of equilibria according to the possible strategies of banks and firms. On this ground, as already remarked, the followers of the circuit approach can count on high-level forerunners. Wicksell, after presenting a complete model of a monetary economy, totally abandons the neoclassical idea of a unique equilibrium position in which consumer sovereignty prevails. His conclusion is that a hypothetical agreement between firms and banks tending to set the money interest rate below what he names the 'natural' rate, can bring about a 'lengthening of the average period of production', thus imposing on consumers an amount of forced saving and creating an extra amount of profits to be distributed between banks and firms at the expense of consumers (Wicksell 1936 [1898] chapter 9, appendix B).

Another clear forerunner of the circulation approach is J.A. Schumpeter, who sharply refused the principle of consumer sovereignty (Schumpeter 1939, chapter 3, §A: 73–4). The same author, when tracing the image of a banker who takes the crucial decision whether or not to allow a firm to embark on an investment, used to emphasise the power of the banking sector (Schumpeter 1934 [1911], chapters 2 and 3, §1). In a different context, Keynes himself, who didn't always give an equally relevant role to the banks, in a 1937 article in which he regrets his neglect of the analysis of the supply of money in the *General Theory*, recognises that, while speculators and *rentiers* bear the responsibility for demand failures and for the consequent phases of prolonged depression, the banks, by creating means of payment, are able to exert an even greater power on the working of the economic system (Keynes 1973b [1937]: 210–11).

## 9.4   The formation of profits

In the neoclassical perspective the distribution of income follows the marginal productivity principle, according to which each resource receives a share of the total product proportionate to its contribution to aggregate production. The neoclassical school devoted great efforts to building a theoretical construction corresponding to such a strictly meritocratic criterion and to showing that such a construction is logically consistent as well as adequately realistic. The whole doctrine of the marginal productivity of distribution no less than the marginal theory of production was built in view of this aim.

The neoclassical doctrine of profit is a clear example of the marginal approach. According to the more rigorous version of the theory of general economic equilibrium (the one presented by Léon Walras in his *Elements of Pure Economics*), in a perfectly competitive equilibrium, profits should disappear. In a competitive market, an entrepreneur should operate without profits or losses and his remuneration should be viewed as a reward for the work performed as a co-ordinator of production. As Marshall would say, the reward of entrepreneurs is no more than the remuneration of a fourth factor of production to be added to the traditional three (labour, land and capital) and called the 'organisation' (Marshall, 1961 [1920]: 138–9). If it happens, and it usually does happen, that even in a perfectly competitive market entrepreneurs are present who enjoy extra profits, this is due to the presence of strictly personal abilities and their profit should be read as the reward of a special kind of labour. In Marshall's reading, the marginal entrepreneur, the less efficient one, the one whose receipts barely cover costs, doesn't get any profit. He is the only one to whom the Walrasian rule (no profits, no losses) literally applies.

Followers of the circulation approach reject the marginal theory of distribution with radical motivations. As shown in the preceding chapters, according to the circulation approach, not only are profits commonly present, but they are totally independent of the abilities or the performance of the entrepreneur. Profits are only due to the fact that the firms, being able to enter the commodities market as buyers with unlimited purchasing power, and being sure of getting back the whole of their expenses by selling commodities or issuing securities, are also able to acquire the share of real product satisfying their production and investment plans.

## 9.5 The nature of interest

An equally deep divergence prevails between the circulation approach and the dominant doctrine regarding the relations between profits and interest.

In the neoclassical doctrine, while profit, if present, corresponds to a special ability of the entrepreneur, interest is viewed as the reward of savers for having advanced the resources required for the acquisition of fixed capital. Interest is therefore the reward of the capitalists' saving (or abstinence, or waiting). In fact, in equilibrium, the rate of interest should be equal both to the marginal time preference of savers and to the marginal productivity of investment. The total interest payments made by firms to savers should be proportional to the amount of saving supplied and therefore to the amount of capital invested by the firms. In formal terms, total product is defined as a function of the quantities of resources being used, the different resources being reduced, by way of simplification, to quantities of labour $N$ and capital $K$:

$X = f(N, K)$,

while the reward of each resource (real wage or real interest) equals the marginal product of the same resource:

$\delta X/\delta N = w/p; \quad \delta X/\delta K = r.$

The total remuneration of capital, and therefore the financial burden falling on the firms and paid to savers, is proportional to the amount of fixed capital invested. In the neoclassical model, interest paid to the banks doesn't appear. This may be due to the fact that, wages being not advanced but paid after the productive process is over, firms are not held to pay the wage bill in advance and therefore need not make recourse to bank credit for an equivalent amount (see §2.3).

In the circulation approach the reverse is true. Interest is not paid to savers only but also to banks, it is paid on bank loans in existence and not on fixed capital invested, and is in no way related to the productivity of the means of production employed. In the circulation approach, interest originates not from saving or abstinence but from the fact that in a monetary economy, access to money and credit is a key factor. The banks, being the producers of money and credit, enjoy a privileged position allowing them to get hold of a share of total product (this aspect was emphasised by Neisser (1928: 13)).

## 9.6   The nature of money

According to the circulation approach, banks and firms should be viewed not only as distinct but also as conflicting sectors. Money in circulation appears as originating from negotiations taking place between banks and firms in the credit market and, in contrast to the dominant view, is defined as a *strictly endogenous magnitude*.

The analysis of a monetary economy clarifies a misunderstanding common to most authors of the neoclassical school, a misunderstanding consisting in thinking on the one hand that liquidity supplied by the banks originates from saving and on the other hand that it is used for financing investment. The preceding analysis shows clearly instead that bank finance has nothing to do either with saving or with investment. Bank finance is not related to savings because bank loans are made possible by liquidity advanced by the banks themselves, who don't draw on any previous income. Nor are bank loans related to investment because initial finance required by producers has to cover the whole cost of producing both consumer goods and investment goods. Therefore, the possibility that firms can carry out their production plans is not in the hands of savers and of their willingness to supply an adequate amount of saving, but rather in the hands of the banks and of their willingness to supply the required liquidity. Under this viewpoint, as already remarked, the monetary theory of production is directly related to Schumpeter's teaching and to his theory of the banker as the ultimate judge of the entrepreneur's plans (Schumpeter 1934 [1911] chapter 2; Messori 1984). Keynes himself, who, as we know, in his *General Theory* had neglected the role performed by the banks in financing the economy, on revisiting the problem a few years later emphasised the requirement of an initial bank loan (Keynes 1973b [1937]: 248).

## 9.7 Investment finance

Newly produced capital goods can be purchased by the firms themselves if they decide to make new investments; or they can be (indirectly) purchased by households if they place their financial saving in securities issued by the firms. As previously said, according to the circulation approach, purchases made by the firms in the commodities market give rise to a forced saving imposed on households. The result is that investments always find their counterpart in aggregate saving, be it voluntary or forced saving. Such saving is in fact the final finance of investment (Keynes 1973a [1936]: 81ff.).

Forced saving disappears only in special cases, when voluntary savings of households are equal to investments planned by the firms. In this case firms make no profits and investment is wholly financed by issuing securities on the financial market. One might then say that the financial market plays the role of financing investment, while in all other cases the role of the financial market is more correctly defined as one of channelling to the firms the monetary savings of households.

## 9.8  Self-financing

Self-financing of firms is often mentioned in the literature as a possible source of finance. The most common opinion is that financially sound firms should be able to finance their own investments either by means of self-financing or by selling equities to savers. The presence of a high long-term debt is often considered a symptom of financial weakness.

In order to analyse the problem in the perspective of the circulation approach, let us assume an economic system formed by the private sector only, government expenditure and government debt being absent. In a similar system, the money stock is wholly formed by a debt owed by firms to the central bank. The assets and liabilities accounts of the firms are consequently extremely simple. The assets are plants and machinery plus possible inventories of semi-finished products. The liabilities are:

a)   the stock of securities outstanding;
b)   the debt to the banks, equal by definition to the liquid holdings of wage earners;

c)   if the value of the assets is higher than the value of the stock in the hands of the public, a part of the assets forms the firm's own capital, originating from accumulated profits. This last entry is the counterpart of self-financing.

The conclusion can be drawn that if we consider the initial financial requirement of the firms (namely the means of payment required for purchasing the means of production), self-financing can be ruled out, since initial finance can only come from bank debt. If we consider instead the problem of financing investment, self-financing is present to the extent to which firms have earned and accumulated profits.

The same is true, even if with slight alterations, if the government sector is present. As previously said (§5.4), the presence of deficit spending reduces the bank debt of firms and may allow firms to accumulate liquid holdings and to become partially independent of the banks. In this case, self-financing may play the role not only of a source of final finance for investment but also of a source of initial finance. However, as it clearly appears, this happens because the government sector has gone into debt with the central bank and, by means of deficit spending, has passed on liquidity to the private sector.

Similar remarks apply equally well to the case of a single firm. As previously pointed out more than once, in principle any single firm is able to make money profits and therefore can have access to self-financing for its own requirements of initial finance. Of course, if one firm has initial finance of its own and is financing part of its own expenditure, there must be at least one other agent having a budget deficit, be it another firm incurring losses or the government sector incurring a deficit.

Anyhow, it appears clearly that, if we consider the firms sector as a whole and we abstract from the presence of a government deficit, self-financing can only appear in the form of accumulated profits, never as the presence of available initial finance. Such conclusions raise doubts on the distinction, suggested in the past by J.R. Hicks, between a so-called pure auto-sector, based on direct possession of liquid assets, and an overdraft sector, working by means of credit and bank loans and relying only on its own borrowing power (Hicks 1974, chapter 2: 50ff.).[1]

## 9.9   Economic crises

Followers of the circulation approach admit two origins of an economic crisis, relating respectively to the phases of opening and closure of the process of money circulation. The reasoning will be made simpler by starting with the analysis of the closure of the money circuit, since this is a more familiar problem, being amply analysed in Keynesian macroeconomics.

As already noted, firms can be considered to be financially in equilibrium any time they retrieve, by selling commodities or by issuing securities, the whole of the liquidity borrowed from the banks. A first case to be considered is an increase in liquid holdings in the possession of savers. We know that in this case the firm's bank debt is increased. Since, beyond given limits, the banks might consider it inadvisable to increase loans granted to the firms, their decision might bring about an economic crisis. This possibility cannot be ruled out, but it can be considered improbable. An increase in liquidity preference should induce a generalised increase in bank debts of all firms (this is one of the cases of economic crisis considered by Keynes in his *General Theory*); and if the increase in bank debts is a really general

---

[1] Of course no problem exists when Hicks refers to single sectors. The case is different when Hicks refers to 'a pure auto economy', one in which no overdraft sectors are present and all producers can rely on the possession of liquid reserves and money (Hicks 1974: 51).

phenomenon, it might be clear to the banks that it is not due to errors in management of single firms, but rather to an increase in the demand for money by the public. If this is the case, banks should remember that their role is precisely to satisfy the demand for liquid holdings coming from the public and should grant the firms the higher loans they require. It should be remembered also that as typical an anti-Keynesian scholar as F.A. Hayek agreed that the banks should grant higher loans whenever liquidity preference increases (Hayek 1978).

The conclusion may of course be different if cases of isolated firms are considered, since even if firms, considered as a whole, are financially in equilibrium, there may be single firms earning profits and others suffering corresponding losses. If this is the case, the banks might cut finance to the firms whose bank debt is increasing beyond average. The situation might be re-equilibrated by means of transactions taking place among single firms, in that firms making profits might grant credit to firms making losses, or even decide to acquire them. If this doesn't happen, the firms making losses might be forced to reduce the level of their activity for lack of bank credit. The possibility of balancing profits and losses would thus no longer be present, the general activity level would fall and a general crisis might take place.

Let us now consider the case of a crisis due to factors acting in the opening phase of the monetary circuit. Such factors have equally been considered by Keynes. To begin with, banks may refuse to satisfy the credit requirements of the firms, this being an example of what Keynes, as recalled above, named 'the power of the banks'. A second possibility is that the firms themselves may decide to reduce their activity levels. In both cases a depression cannot be avoided. It should be emphasised that in such cases the Pigou effect, an effect that in the neoclassical perspective should allow a way out of the depression, doesn't operate. In fact a fall in the level of activity can well be followed, as Pigou would have it, by a general decline in wages and prices, which (and this is the substance of the Pigou effect) would clearly produce an increase in the real value of agents' money holdings. But if the depression originates from an autonomous decision of the firms to reduce their activity levels and consequently to reduce the amount of bank loans demanded, the nominal money holdings will decrease as prices fall and no Pigou effect will be started (Keynes 1973a [1936]: 266).

Under this aspect, a difference should be pointed out between the two possible cases of a depression mentioned so far. In the first case (factors acting at the closure of the monetary circuit) the depression originates precisely from the formation of liquid holdings, be it liquid holdings of savers or of firms making profits. Declining prices then do produce an increase in the real value of agents' liquid wealth, which can be a prerequisite for an increase in aggregate demand. In the second case (factors acting at the opening of the monetary circuit), the decision of firms to reduce the level of activity produces, along with declining prices, a decline both in loans granted to the firms and of the money stock in existence. The economy is therefore in the situation in which, as Keynes said in criticising the Pigou effect even before it was suggested, 'if the money stock is itself a function of the level of prices and wages, there is little to be hoped in this direction' (Keynes 1973a [1936], chapter 19: 266).

## 9.10 The problem of 'financirisation'

It is a common observation that nowadays savers and speculators tend to privilege financial placements as compared to productive initiatives. A dominant opinion is that the increasing weight of finance depends on an alteration of agents' preferences and more specifically on the fact that investors are becoming less and less risk lovers and increasingly risk averse. The consequence is that agents in possession of liquid resources, instead of using them for hiring labour and setting up a process of production, prefer to lend them and get a safer income in the form of interest payments.

The analysis of the circulation approach shows that, for finance to increase its weight as compared to production, a fall in entrepreneurial spirit is not enough and that additional technical factors are needed. More precisely:

a)    A first condition is the presence of firms having earned profits not only in kind (which would only be a case of self-financed investment) but in the form of money. As previously shown, this can happen only if at the same time other agents are incurring losses. This is tantamount to saying that a considerable increase in financial activity to the detriment of real production can only take place in the presence of disequilibria in the balance sheets of single agents: for instance when whole groups of firms suffer conspicuous losses while other groups earn corresponding profits; or in the presence of a considerable government deficit. A simple decrease in the propensity to risk, while possibly producing a fall in activity levels, cannot give rise to an increase in finance over production. A typical case of such disequilibria is the case of government deficit creating corresponding profits in the private sector.

b)    A second condition is also necessary, namely that agents in debt towards the banks be prepared to obtain loans from agents endowed with liquid holdings, thus replacing bank debt by debt towards other agents. This can easily happen when the government tries to finance its own deficit by issuing new securities. The same can happen whenever a credit squeeze occurs and firms having financial problems, and unable to get the required amount of credit from a bank, try to take advantage of liquidity holdings existing in the non-banking sector. It is after all a well-known consequence of a credit squeeze that a reduction in the money stock, or in its rate of growth, gives rise to an increase in the velocity of circulation.

The conclusion of the preceding remarks is that, according to the circulation approach, the so-called phenomenon of an increasing weight of the financial sector is explained not so much by a decline in entrepreneurship, but rather by a high government deficit coupled to a credit squeeze.

# References

Arestis, Ph. 1997, *Money, Pricing, Distribution and Economic Integration*, London, Macmillan

Arrow, K.J. and Hahn, F.H. 1971, *General Competitive Analysis*, Edinburgh, Oliver & Boyd

Barrère, A. 1979, *Déséquilibres économiques et contre-révolution keynésienne*, Paris, Economica

Barrère, A. (ed.) 1985, *Keynes aujourd'hui*, Paris, Economica
1988a, *The Foundations of Keynesian Analysis*, London, Macmillan
1988b, *Money, Credit and Prices in Keynesian Perspective*, London, Macmillan

Benetti, C. 1991, 'Le problème de la valeur de la monnaie: F. Galiani et A. Smith', in Rosier, M. (ed.), *Le marché chez A.Smith*, Paris, l'Harmattan, pp. 105–18

Benetti, C. and Cartelier, J. 1990, 'Monnaie et formation des grandeurs économiques', in Cartelier, J. (ed.), *La formation des grandeurs économiques*, Paris, Presses Universitaires de France, pp. 323–53

Bernanke, B.S. and Blinder, A.S. 1988, 'Credit money and aggregate demand', *American Economic Review*, 78: 435–9

Berti, L. 1987, 'Alle origini della teoria monetaria contemporanea. Il contributo di Gunnar Myrdal', Introduction to the Italian translation of Myrdal 1939: *L'equilibrio monetario*, Rome, Instituto dell'Enciclopedia Italiana
1992, 'Sulla nozione di economia monetaria', *Problemi del socialismo*, 1: 3–11

Blinder, A.S. and Solow, R. 1974, *Economics of Public Finance*, Washington, DC, Brookings Institution

Bossone, B. 2001, 'Circuit theory of banking and finance', *Journal of Banking and Finance*, 25: 857–90

Bresciani-Turroni, C. 1936, 'The theory of saving', *Economica*, 3: 1–23, 162–81

Cannan, E. 1921, 'The meaning of bank deposits', *Economica*, 1: 28–36

Cartelier, J. 1996, 'Payment systems and dynamics in a monetary economy', in Deleplace and Nell, pp. 200–38

   2001, 'La coordination en déséquilibre. Loi de l'offre et de la demande ou régulation monétaire', in Cartelier, J. and Frydman, R.(eds.), *L'économie hors d'équilibre*, Paris, Economica, pp. 151–66

Cencini, A. 1984, *Time and the Macroeconomic Analysis of Income*, London, Pinter

Cencini, A. and Schmitt, B. 1992, 'Per la creazione di uno spazio monetario europeo', in Chopard, R. (ed.), *Europa 93*, Bellinzona, Meta Edizioni, pp. 99–136

Cesarano, F. 1995, 'The new monetary economics and the theory of money', *Journal of Economic Behavior and Organization*, 26: 445–55

Cesaroni, G. 2001, 'The finance motive, the Keynesian theory of the rate of interest and the investment multiplier', *European Journal of the History of Economic Thought*, 8: 58–74

Chick, V. 1986, 'The evolution of the banking system and the theory of saving, investment and interest', *Economies et Sociétés*, Série Monnaie et Production, 3: 111–26

   1995, 'Is there a case for post Keynesian economics?', *Scottish Journal of Political Economy*, 42, 1: 20–36

Clower, R.W. 1977, 'The anatomy of monetary theory', *American Economic Review, Papers and Proceedings*, 67: 206–12

Clower, R.W. (ed.) 1969, *Monetary Theory*, Harmondsworth, Penguin

Debreu, G. 1959, *Theory of Value*, New York, Wiley

De Brunhoff, S. 1976 [1967], *Marx on Money*, New York, Urizen Books

Deleplace, G. and Nell, E. (eds.) 1996, *Money in Motion. The Post-Keynesian and Circulation Approaches*, New York, Macmillan

De Vecchi, N. 1993, *Entrepreneurs, Institutions and Economic Change. The Economic Thought of J. A. Schumpeter 1905– 1925*, Aldershot, Edward Elgar

De Viti De Marco, A. 1885, *Moneta e prezzi*, Città di Castello, Lapi 1990 [1934], *La funzione della banca*, Turin, Utet

Dillard, D. 1980, 'A monetary theory of production. Keynes and the institutionalists', *Journal of Economic Issues*, 24: 255–73

Eboli, M. 1991, 'The finance of fixed and working capital. An exercise in stock-flow modelling', *Studi economici*, 46: 77–104

Edgeworth, F.Y. 1888, 'The mathematical theory of banking', *Journal of the Royal Statistical Society*, 51: 113–27

Fanno, M. 1992 [1933], *La teoria del credito e della circolazione*, ed. A. Graziani and R. Realfonzo, Naples, E.S.I.
    1995 [1912], *The Money Market*, with forewords by A. Graziani and M. Morishima, London, Macmillan

Ferrara, F. 1961 [1856], 'Della moneta e dei suoi surrogati', Preface to *Biblioteca dell'Economista*, vol. 5, now in *Opere complete*, vol. 5, Rome, Bancaria, 1961, pp. 3–35

Fisher, I. 1896, *Appreciation and Interest*, Publications of the American Economic Association, vol. 11, no. 4, New York, Macmillan
    1930, *The Theory of Interest*, New York, Macmillan
    1963 [1911], *The Purchasing Power of Money*, New York, A.M. Kelley

Fontana, G. 2000, 'Post Keynesians and circuitists on money and uncertainty. An attempt at generality', *Journal of Post Keynesian Economics*, 23: 27–48
    2001, 'Rethinking endogenous money. A constructive interpretation of the debate between accommodationists and structuralists', Discussion Paper, University of Leeds, Economics Department, January

Galiani, F. 1780, *Della Moneta*, Naples, Stamperia Simoniana (1st edn, n.p., 1750)

Giacomin, A. 1994, 'Power and trade in the economy of the ancien régime', *Jahrbuch für Wirtschaftsgeschichte*, 6: 131–54

Godley, W. 1990, 'Tempo, rendimenti crescenti e istituzioni in macroeconomia', in Biasco, S., Roncaglia, A. and Salvati, M. (eds.), *Istituzioni e mercato nello sviluppo economico. Saggi in onore di P. Sylos Labini*, Bari, Laterza, pp. 69–94

Godley, W. and Cripps, F. 1981, *Macroeconomics*, London, Fontana

Graziani, A. 1983, 'Interesse reale e interesse monetario. Storia di una controversia', *Rivista milanese di economia*, 6: 77–108

1984, 'The debate on Keynes' finance motive', *Economic Notes*, 1: 5–32

1987, 'Economia Keynesiana e teoria del circuito', in Gandolfo, G. and Marzano, F. (eds.), *Keynesian Theory, Planning Models, and Quantitative Economics*, Milan, Giuffré, pp. 57–76

1989, *The Theory of the Monetary Circuit*, London, Thames Papers in Political Economy (also in *Economies et Sociétés*, Série Monnaie et Production (1990), 7: 7–36)

1991, 'La théorie keynésienne de la monnaie et le financement de l'économie', *Economie appliquée*, 44, 1: 25–41

1994, 'Real wages and the loans–deposits controversy', *Economie appliquée*, 1: 31–46

1996, 'Money as purchasing power and money as a stock of wealth in Keynesian economic thought', in Deleplace and Nell, pp. 200–38

1998, 'A note on Hayek's macroeconomic equilibrium', in Michon, F. (ed.), *L'économie: une science pour l'homme et la société*, Paris, Publications de la Sorbonne, pp. 105–16

Hagemann, H. and Rühl, C. 1987, 'N. Johannsen's early analysis of the savings–investment process and the multiplier', *Studi economici*, 42: 99–144

Hahn, F.H. 1982, *Money and Inflation*, Oxford, Blackwell

Hahn, L.A. 1920, *Volkswirtschaftliche Theorie des Bankkredits*, Tübingen, J.C.B. Mohr

1954, 'Intervention', in Weber, A. (ed.), *Bankkredit und Langfristigen Investitionen*, Berlin, Duncker & Humblot

Halevi, J. and Taouil, R. 1998, 'On a post-Keynesian stream from France and Italy. The circuit approach', University of Sydney, Department of Economics, Working Papers in Economics, no. 98–08

Hansson, B. 1992, 'Forced saving', in Newman, P., Milgate, M. and Eatwell, J. (eds.), *The New Palgrave Dictionary of Money and Finance*, vol. 2, London, Macmillan, pp. 140–1

Hawtrey, R. 1923, *Currency and Credit*, London, Longmans, Green & Co.

1927, *The Gold Standard in Theory and Practice*, London, Longmans, Green & Co. (5th edn, 1947)

1931, 'Credit', in *Encyclopaedia of the Social Sciences*, vol. 4, New York, Macmillan, pp. 545–50

Hayek, F. A. 1932, 'The development of the doctrine of forced saving', *Quarterly Journal of Economics*, 47: 123–33 (reprinted in *Profits, Interest and Investment*, London, Routledge & Kegan Paul, 1939, pp. 183–97)

1933, *Monetary Theory and the Trade Cycle*, London, Jonathan Cape

1935, *Prices and Production*, London, Routledge & Kegan Paul, 2nd edn

1978, *Denationalization of Money*, London, Institute of Economic Affairs

Heinsohn, G. and Steiger, O. 1983, 'Private property, debts and interest, or: The origins of money and the rise and fall of monetary economies', *Studi economici*, 38: 3–56

1996, *Eigentum, Zins und Geld. Ungelöste Rätsel der Wirtschaftswissenschaft*, Reinbek, Rohwolt (2nd edn, Marburg, 2002)

2000, 'The property theory of interest and money', in Smithin, pp. 67–100

2001, 'Property titles as the clue to a successful transformation', in *Verplichtungsökonomik. Eigentum, Freiheit und Haftung in der Geldwirtschaft*, Marburg, Metropolis Verlag, pp. 203–20

Helfferich, K. 1919, *Das Geld*, 4th edn, Leipzig, C.L. Hirschfeld (1st edn 1903)

Hicks, J.R. 1933, 'Gleichgewicht und Konjunktur', *Zeitschrift für Nationalökonomie*, 4: 441–55 (English translation, slightly abridged: 'Equilibrium and the cycle', in Hicks, J., *Money, Interest, and Wages*, Oxford, Blackwell, 1982, pp. 28–41)

1974, *The Crisis in Keynesian Economics*, Oxford, Blackwell

1989, *A Market Theory of Money*, Oxford, Clarendon Press

Howells, P. 2001, 'Real balance effects and endogenous money', paper presented at the Conference on Endogenous Money, Berlin, March

Jannaccone, P. 1946, *Moneta e lavoro*, Turin, Utet

Kaldor, N. 1956, 'Alternative theories of distribution', *Review of Economic Studies*, 23: 83–100 (reprinted in *Essays on Value and Distribution*, London, Duckworth, 1980, pp. 209–36)

1985, 'How monetarism failed', *Challenge*, 28: 4–13

Kalecki, M. 1990 [1933], 'Essay on business cycle theory', in Kalecki 1990–91, vol. 1, pp. 67–81 (first Polish edition 1933)

## 164    References

1990–91, *Collected Works of Michael Kalecki*, Oxford, Clarendon Press, 2 vols.

1991 [1942], 'A theory of profits', *Economic Journal*, 52: 258–67 (reprinted in Kalecki 1990–91, vol. 2, pp. 151–61)

Keynes, J.M. 1971 [1913], *Indian Currency and Finance*, London, Macmillan

1971 [1930], *A Treatise on Money*, London, Macmillan (*Collected Writings of J.M. Keynes*, vols. 5 and 6, London, Macmillan, 1971)

1973a [1936], *The General Theory of Employment, Interest, and Money*, London, Macmillan (*Collected Writings of J.M. Keynes*, vol. 7, London, Macmillan, 1973)

1973b [1937], 'Alternative theories of the rate of interest', *Economic Journal*, 64: 241–52 (*Collected Writings of J.M. Keynes*, vol. 14, London, Macmillan, 1973, pp. 201–15)

1973c [1937], 'The ex-ante theory of the rate of interest', *Economic Journal*, 64: 663–9 (*Collected Writings of J.M. Keynes*, vol. 14, London, Macmillan, 1973, pp. 215–23)

1973d [1937], 'The general theory of employment', *Quarterly Journal of Economics*, 51: 209–23 (*Collected Writings of J.M. Keynes*, vol. 14, London, Macmillan, 1973, pp. 109–23)

1983 [1914], Review of 'A. M. Innes, What is Money?', *Economic Journal* (*Collected Writings of J.M. Keynes*, vol. 11, London, Macmillan, 1983, pp. 404–6)

Knapp, G.F. 1924 [1905], *The State Theory of Money*, London, Macmillan

Kregel, J.A. 1973, *The Reconstruction of Political Economy. An Introduction to Post-Keynesian Economics*, London, Macmillan

1986, 'Shylock or Hamlet: Are There Bulls and Bears in the Circuit?', *Economies et Sociétés*, Série Monnaie et Production, 3: 11–22

Lahn, J.J.O. 1903, *Der Kreislauf des Geldes*, Berlin, Puttkammer & Mühlbrecht

Lavoie, M. 1987, 'Monnaie et production. Une synthèse de la théorie du circuit', *Economies et Sociétés*, Série Monnaie et Production, 4: 65–102

1992, 'Jacques Le Bourva's theory of endogeneous credit-money', *Review of Political Economy*, 4: 436–46

1993, *Foundations of Post-Keynesian Economic Analysis*, Aldershot, Edward Elgar

1996, 'Monetary policy in an economy with endogenous credit money', in Deleplace and Nell, pp. 532–45

Le Bourva, J. 1962, 'Création de la monnaie et multiplicateur du crédit', *Revue économique*, 23: 243–82

Leijonhufvud, A. and Heymann, D. 1991, 'Money and the price level', University of Trento, *Annali del Dipartimento di Economia. A Supplement to Economia e Banca*, 4: 1–37

Lindhal, E. 1930, *Penningpolitikens medel*, Malmö, Forlagsaktienbolaget (English translation in Lindhal, E., *Studies in the Theory of Money and Capital*, London, Allen & Unwin, 1939, part II)

Lüken Klassen, M. 1998, 'Dominanzverhältnisse in der Geldwirtschaft', in Schelkle, W. and Nitsch, M. (eds.), *Rätsel Geld*, Marburg, Metropolis Verlag, 2nd edn, pp. 63–76

Lundberg, E. 1937, *Studies in the Theory of Economic Expansion*, London, King & Sons

Machlup, F. 1932, 'The liquidity of short-term capital', *Economica*, 12: 271–84

1943, 'Forced or induced saving: an exploration into its synonyms and homonyms', *Review of Economics and Statistics*, 25: 26–39

Mankiw, N.G. 1992, *Macroeconomics*, New York, Worth Publishers Inc.

Marget, A.W. 1966 [1938], *The Theory of Prices*, New York, A.M. Kelley

Marshall, A. 1961 [1920], *Principles of Economics*, edited by C.W. Guillebaud, London, Macmillan

1975 [1870], *The Early Economic Writings of A. Marshall*, edited by J.K. Whitaker, London, Macmillan

McCallum, B.T. 1985, 'Bank deregulation, accounting systems of exchange and the unit of account: a critical review', *Carnegie-Rochester Conference Series on Public Policy*, 23: 13–46

Menger, C. 1892, 'On the origin of money', *Economic Journal*, 2: 239–55

Messori, M. 1985, 'Le circuit de la monnaie. Acquis et problèmes non résolus', in Arena, R. and Graziani, A. (eds.), *Production, circulation et monnaie*, Paris, Presses Universitaires de France, pp. 120–36

1988, 'Agenti e mercati in uno schema periodale', in Messori, M. (ed.), *Moneta e produzione*, Turin, Einaudi, pp. 303–14

Messori, M. (ed.) 1984, *J.A. Schumpeter. Antologia di scritti*, Bologna, Il Mulino

Mill, J.S. 1909 [1848], *Principles of Political Economy*, edited by W.J. Ashley, London, Longmans, Green & Co.

Modigliani, F. and Cohn, R.A. 1979, 'Inflation, rational valutation and the market', *Financial Analysts Journal*, 35: 27–40

Modigliani, F. and Papademos L. 1990, 'The supply of money and the control of nominal income', in Friedman, B.M. and Hahn, F.H. (eds.), *Handbook of Monetary Economics*, Amsterdam, North-Holland, pp. 398–494

Moore, B.J. 1983, 'Unpacking the post-Keynesian black box: bank lending and the money supply', *Journal of Post-Keynesian Economics*, 5: 537–56

1984, 'Keynes and the endogeneity of the money stock', *Studi economici*, 39: 23–70

Myrdal, G. 1939, *Monetary Equilibrium*, London, W. Hodge

Neisser, H. 1928, *Der Tauschwert des Geldes*, Jena, G. Fischer Verlag

1931, 'Kreislauf des Geldes', *Weltwirtschaftliches Archiv*, 33: 365–408

1950 [1934], 'General overproduction. A study of Say's law of markets', *Journal of Political Economy*, 42: 433–65 (reprinted abridged in *Readings in Business Cycle Theory*, American Economic Society, 1950, pp. 385–404)

Padoa Schioppa, T. 1989, 'International payment systems: the function begets the organ', Bank of Italy, *Economic Bulletin*, 9: 67–74

Palley, T.I. 1997, 'Endogenous money and the business cycle', *Journal of Economics*, 65: 133–49

Pantaleoni, M. 1898, *Pure Economics*, London, Macmillan (reprinted New York, Kelley & Millman, 1957)

Parguez, A. 1975, *Monnaie et macroéconomie*, Paris, Economica

1981, 'Ordre social, monnaie, et régulation', *Economie Appliquée*, 2–3: 383–448

1984, 'La dynamique de la monnaie', *Economies et Sociétés*, Série Monnaie et Production, 1: 83–118

1985, 'La Théorie Générale: la révolution inachevée dans la théorie du capital et du revenu', in Barrère, pp. 257–75

Parguez, A. and Seccareccia, M. 2000, 'The credit theory of money: the monetary circuit approach', in Smithin, pp. 101–23

Patinkin, D. 1965, *Money, Interest, and Prices*, 2nd edn, New York, Harper & Row

Patinkin, D. and Steiger, O. 1989, 'In search of the veil of money and the neutrality of money', *Scandinavian Journal of Economics*, 91: 131–46

Poulon, F. 1982, *Macroéconomie approfondie*, Paris, Cujas

Realfonzo, R. 1998, *Money and Banking. Theory and Debate 1900–1940*, Aldershot, Edward Elgar

Riese, H. 1992, 'Bagehot versus Goodhart. Warum eine Zentralbank Geschäftsbanken braucht', University of Bremen, Postkeynesianische Forschungsgruppe, working paper no. 22

1998, 'Geld: Das letzte Rätsel der Nationalökonomie', in Schelkle, W. and Nitsch, M. (eds.), *Rätsel Geld*, Marburg, Metropolis Verlag, 2nd edn

Robertson, D.H. 1926, *Banking Policy and the Price Level*, London, King & Son

1928, 'Theories of banking policy', *Economica* (1928): 131–46 (reprinted in *Economic Essays and Addresses*, London, P.S. King & Son)

1937, 'Alternative theories of the rate of interest. Three rejoinders', *Economic Journal*, 47: 428–36

Robinson, J. 1956, *The Accumulation of Capital*, London, Macmillan

Sawyer, M. 1985, 'Finance, money, and unemployment', Berlin, International Institute of Management, Discussion Paper no. 11

Schlesinger, K. 1914, *Theorie der Geld und Kreditwirtschaft*, Munich, Duncker & Humblot (English translation of ch. 3, 'Basic principles of the money economy', *International Economic Papers*, vol. 9, London, Macmillan, 1959, pp. 20–38)

Schmitt, B. 1972, *Macroeconomic Theory*, Albeuve, Editions Castella

1975, *Théorie unitaire de la monnaie, nationale et internationale*, Albeuve, Castella

1984, *Inflation, chômage et malformations du capital*, Paris, Economica

## 168   References

1996, 'A new paradigm for the determination of money prices', in Deleplace and Nell, pp. 104–38

Schmitt B. and Greppi, S. 1996, 'The national economy studied as a whole', in Deleplace and Nell, pp. 341–64

Schneider, E. 1962, *Money, Income and Employment*, London, Allen & Unwin

Schumpeter, J.A. 1934 [1911], *The Theory of Economic Development*, Cambridge, MA, Harvard University Press (1st German edn, Munich, Duncker & Humblot, 1911)

1939, *Business Cycles*, New York, McGraw-Hill

1954, *History of Economic Analysis*, Oxford, Oxford University Press

1970, *Das Wesen des Geldes*, edited by F.K. Mann, Göttingen, Vandenhoeck & Ruprecht

Screpanti, E. 1993, *Capital accumulation and the monetary circuit*, Rome, CNR/IDSE

Simiand, F. 1932, *Le salaire*, Parigi, Alcan

Sismondi, J. Ch. 1810, *Du papier monnaie et des moyens de le supprimer*, Weimar, Landes-Industrie-Comptoir

1991 [1819], *New Principles of Political Economy*, New Brunswick, NJ, Transaction Publishers

Smith, A. 1993 [1776], *An Inquiry into the Nature and Causes of the Wealth of Nations*, Oxford, Oxford University Press

Smithin, J. 1994, *Controversies in Monetary Economics*, Aldershot, Edward Elgar

Smithin, J. (ed.) 2000, *What is Money?*, London, Routledge

Stiglitz, J. 1999, 'Towards a new paradigm for monetary economics', Milan, Università Bocconi, Mattioli Lecture Series, mimeo

Studart, R. 1995, *Investment Finance in Economic Development*, London, Routledge

Sylos Labini, P. 1948, 'Saggio dell'interesse e reddito sociale', Rome, Accademia Nazionale dei Lincei, *Rendiconti*, Series VIII, vol. 3, nos. 11–12

Tobin, J. 1963, 'Commercial banks as creators of money', in Carson, D. (ed.), *Banking and Monetary Studies*, Homewood, IL, Irwin, pp. 408–19

1980, 'Asset accumulation and economic activity', Oxford, Blackwell

1982a, 'The commercial banking firm', *Scandinavian Journal of Economics*, 84: 495–530

1982b, 'Money and finance in the macroeconomic process', *Journal of Money, Credit, and Banking*, 14: 171–204

1986, 'On the welfare macroeconomics of government financial policy', *Scandinavian Journal of Economics*, 88: 9–24

1992, 'Money', in Newman, P., Milgate, M. and Eatwell, J. (eds.), *The New Palgrave Dictionary of Money and Finance*, vol. 2, London, Macmillan, pp. 770–9

Thornton, H. 1939 [1811], 'Two speeches on the Bullion Report', reprinted as an appendix to Hayek, F.A. (ed.), *An Enquiry into the Nature and Effects of the Paper Credit in Great Britain*, London, LSE, 1939, pp. 335–78

Villieu, P. 1993, 'Les modèles à encaisses préalables: un renouveau des fondements microéconomiques de la macroéconomie monétaire?', *Revue d'économie politique*, 103, 5: 613–94

von Mises, L. 1928, *Geldwertstabilisierung und Konjunkturpolitik*, Jena, Fischer Verlag

1934 [1912], *The Theory of Money and Credit*, London, Jonathan Cape

Walras, L. 1954 [1926], *Elements of Pure Economics*, translated by W. Jaffé, London, Allen & Unwin

White, L.H. 1984, 'Competitive monetary reform: a review essay', *Journal of Monetary Economics*, 26: 192–202

Wicksell, K. 1936 [1898], *Interest and Prices*, London, Macmillan, 1936 (1st German edn, Jena, Fischer Verlag, 1898)

Wray, L.R. 1990, *Money and Credit in Capitalist Economies. The Endogenous Money Approach*, Aldershot, Edward Elgar

1993, 'The monetary macroeconomics of D. Dillard', *Journal of Economic Issues*, 27: 547–60

1996, 'Money in the circular flow', in Deleplace and Nell, pp. 440–64

1998, *Understanding Modern Money*, Aldershot, Edward Elgar

# Index